Oh, no! Not Another
Learning Experience!
A Metamorphosis

My Journey

By

Laurie D Wheeler

Laurie D. Wheeler

Oh, no! Not Another Learning Experience
A Metamorphosis
by
Laurie D. Wheeler
Copyright ©Laurie D Wheeler 2019

Genre: Memoir, Metaphysical, Self-Help, Nonfiction, Paranormal

Print edition, first printing December 2019
ISBN: 978-0-578-61675-9

Dedication

I dedicate this book to all of you on the path,
committed to learning, experiencing and growing
who you really are...
For the younger generations who will carry on the
legacy of life
For the ancestors who have gone before and
who will follow
For the people I've encountered along my life's
journey who have encouraged me to follow my path
To my four children, who have
taught me much about love
To my husband, as we do this journey together
sharing our experiences and learning from each
other, you are the one who brings the humor into my
life and helps me smile through the challenges.

Laurie D. Wheeler

Table of Contents

Foreword

I started thinking of writing a book back in the late 90's, knowing what the title would be since that time.

Oh No! Not Another Learning Experience was a bumper sticker given to me by one of my clients early in my practice, and I realized then that it was going to be the title of a book I wanted to write someday.

My vision and passion has always been clear, to share both personally and professionally with those who are curious about the unknown realms, for those who are beginning to wake onto their own spiritual path or those who are on their path and learning each day what it means to be "your authentic self."

It is my hope this book will serve as an example and guidance to those seeking answers to the deep burning questions we can have at times in our lives: *Who am I? What is my life's purpose? Why do I feel different from others? Why do I feel disconnected? Etcetera...*

I remember a regression I was guided through a time ago. I wanted to experience the time of origin when I first felt separated. I was taken to the moment when I separated from Source/Creator and became my own soul. I realized that every soul must have this experience because it is how we evolve. Although I also realize this is an illusion because we are a part of everything, we must consciously remember and feel our true selves on a daily basis.

As I have explored these questions both personally and professionally, it is the quest that led me to find the answers. In the pages following, I share my personal background, my in-depth struggles and accomplishments in the search to find my true soul and acknowledge those that brought me learning and guidance along the way.

Life is both a great pleasure and continued daily reminder of what we are all doing here on this beautiful Earth planet, our connection to the collective consciousness and the greater cosmos. As we learn what this lifetime and our other lives are about, we then can clear and let go of what no longer serve us, allowing us to know more of who we are. When we evolve as souls, moving toward our Oneness, we then can live in the intended world, as the Great Divine Plan.

If you are someone thirsting for answers and searching to find them, I hope you'll explore with me and uncover your unanswered questions...*who are you and what is your purpose?*

Although this is a memoir, a work of creative nonfiction, some of the names have been changed to protect the privacy of certain individuals. This is my story, told purely from my perspective. Conversations and situations are from my memory and are retold to the best of my ability.

Chapter One

While looking for my health,
I found my soul's path...

*A journey of a thousand miles
begins with a single step*

In 1989, I thought my life was going pretty well. We had just sold a small house in New Jersey that my husband and I had been renovating for the last seven years, a fixer upper, and we were excited to finally build the house of our dreams. Having spent many weekends driving through the lower region of Orange County in New York State, searching for the right piece of land, we found thirteen lightly wooded acres in a beautiful farming area. Now, we were ready to pack and make the move.

This region of New York and the surrounding areas had been inhabited, not so long ago, by many Native American tribes. Most of the names of the towns and areas were the same as years gone by and the land was rich and fertile for farming. In fact, this part of the county was undeveloped yet considered to be up-and-coming. It was certainly a prime piece of property on which to build a beautiful home to raise our family. This was going to be the house of our dreams where we were to raise our four children, or so I thought. Growing up in the country—the outdoors with wide-open spaces, surrounded by nature and wildlife—sounded exciting, and we couldn't wait to make it happen.

There was so much to do over the next six months with the transitioning—finishing the last touches of our new home, moving a large family into a new place, and getting the children settled into schools. It was challenging and hectic, but an exciting adventure—all in all, we were happy and looking forward to our new lives.

Shortly after moving in, some of us noticed we were feeling a bit sick often enough that it caught my attention. We had more colds and flus in our family than was usual for us. Now, you might chalk this up to new surroundings and some stress from adjusting — as I did—but the illnesses didn't stop after a considerable time. I couldn't quite put my finger on it, but somehow the situation didn't appear right.

As a little time passed, and after getting to

know our neighbors, we discovered there were quite a number of folks ill in the area. I heard of a family, young and older members, who were all losing their hair. Also, I discovered a few people who had suddenly developed cancerous tumors. In addition to all of that, I learned that many people in the area suffered from digestive disturbances. This all sounded a bit strange to me at the time, but not thinking too much about it, I went on settling into my new life.

One day I decided to take a walk around the corner of our property. There was a woman I had been wanting to meet, a dog breeder who had lived there for many years. Every spring for nine years, she had been unsuccessful in breeding her dogs and she couldn't understand the reason why. Although this struck a chord of mystery within me, I shrugged it off without much further thought.

As time went by, we found out through one of the locals, that the land we lived on was on top of an aquifer. An aquifer is a large underground body of water, much like a lake. It is known that water can flow either up or down hill, or any direction — taking along with it a portion of whatever it flows over, including chemicals.

Another month passed by when I learned through the local farmers there was a crop duster about half a mile up the hill from us. Every spring and summer he would spray the farmlands in our area. I could actually see him fly his small plane overhead as I stood outside in the yard. This was troubling to many of us in the area, as we all thought this couldn't be good for our health; if it were killing insects what could it do to us?

As I explored more of the surrounding

area, I discovered a paint chemical plant about one mile away from where we lived. Remember, I mentioned that water grabs a little of everything it flows over. Now, I had begun piecing together some of what I was learning, and the picture started becoming clearer for me. I actually became very concerned about my family's health at this point. I had also started noticing that my memory wasn't functioning as well as usual and I was only in my early thirties. For example, I was forgetting how to get to places that I should easily remember. I had a part-time job working in the school at this time and couldn't keep from catching colds. My immunity was very compromised. Likewise, my children suffered from upper respiratory illnesses quite frequently. We all experienced digestive issues in one form or another. All of us were enduring odd symptoms and not feeling like our usual selves.

Simultaneous to not feeling well at this time, some strange occurrences began to unfold in and outside of our home. One of my children expressed that when he opened a particular pantry door it felt as if he could be in another place in time. He didn't say too much about this and I attributed it to youthful imagination. Once in a while, in the hallway, several of us would see a dark shadow move across the room. Also, our dog would bark at this certain corner of the living room, for no apparent reason—as if something were there that we couldn't see. None of us understood what this was about, but one thing was for sure, I had never experienced anything like this, and it definitely did not feel normal.

When I would take the dog outside, I felt as though an unseen presence watched me, like there were more than one set of eyes peering at me from the shadows of the trees; yet no one was there. It made me feel very uncomfortable. This bothered me so much that I stopped taking the dog out after dark. My dog, Becky, a rescue dog was part Collie and Shepherd mix and a wonderful watch dog, was always interested in going by this one particular tree behind our home. It was an evergreen tree but an unusual shape from the others on the property, split in odd directions with twisted limbs. My boys built a tree house in its gnarled branches and would ride their ATV around it. There was just something about this tree... it had a compelling energy that drew us to it. We noted that certain parts of our property felt more this way than others.

Each one of these happenings by itself really wasn't anything to be too concerned about and could probably be reasoned away, but when you put it all together…it was both strange and mysterious.

A few years passed and life moved forward, but things weren't as comfortable as we thought they should be. These strange occurrences continued and the issues with our health were troublesome. On top of that, the economy at this time began having difficulties. We made a decision to sell the house for the simple reason that we didn't feel comfortable there any longer. We had an unusual feeling that we didn't belong there or that we shouldn't be there, even though that didn't make complete sense. We thought, *"This had been our dream, so how can it be right to sell it? We had worked so hard to get here…how can we give it up?"*

We put it on the market to sell, but it sat for quite an unusually long time without any serious buyers. Despite being priced right, no one would buy the house. It was a large Colonial home with beautiful gardens that I had planted around the outside. As an artist, I had painted murals on some walls and decorated the interior in a comfortable country flair. Many people who came looking at the house gave great feedback; but when asked why they didn't want to make an offer, no one could give us a well-defined answer. Everyone, including the realtors, were perplexed yet we continued trying. After about ten months of working at selling our home, we wondered if we were doing the right thing. It was very perplexing. Were we to stay or go? It was hard to know what to do.

Late one particular morning, I was home gardening in the backyard while the kids were at school. I was all alone—or so I thought—when an unusual feeling came over me. I felt compelled to walk in the back woods to the very large and oddly shaped evergreen tree—the same one the boys would ride their ATV around and where they had built a tree fort. Due to all the poison ivy there, I usually avoided this area of the woods.

It was as if a voice called to me, yet there was no one around. As I said, the kids were at school and I was alone. I could hear the voice, and feel a sense within that said, "Come back here."

It was sort of eerie to me, but I made my way back toward the tree because this was the area where it felt like the voice was strongest. When I made my way back there and leaned against the tree, within a moment, I felt as if I were in another time — another reality — as if I were dreaming while still awake—like being in a movie but unfamiliar with the scenery.

I immediately thought to myself, *"How*

could this be? What is happening to me? How did I get here?"

As this dream-like state unfolded, I found myself in a sort of funeral setting mourning over a hundred people who had died suddenly. I wondered, *"Who are all of these people and what am I doing here? I don't know any of them,"* yet I could feel all of their sorrow for those they had lost. *"How can this be?"*

The feeling overwhelmed and perplexed me. I had so many questions...I didn't understand any of this.

As a few more moments passed, the scene continued to unfold. This experience was like a movie playing out on a screen, but the screen was inside my head. For a moment, I thought maybe this was a movie I had watched on TV and I wasn't really experiencing this at all. Then, I realized it wasn't something I had seen before in a movie or anything I had read—this was really happening to me.

I was experiencing a time in the past that appeared to be in the 1800's. It was late at night, and a small group of Native American people (a war party) crept into a village where another tribe slept. The war party began attacking and killing the sleeping tribe. Those who had been sleeping and were able to escape, now ran from their homes screaming and wailing, but many were dead. The scene was so horrible—vivid— and I witnessed it all right in front of me—*in my mind*. People ran everywhere, and then as quickly as it had begun; it was all over. The war party left—leaving behind death and destruction.

I experienced this deeply within my whole self, as if I had been a part of the entire happening. The moans of those in sorrow over their lost loved ones penetrated my heart. I felt as if I had sucked it all into me at once—I felt extreme pain and clenched at my heart. I didn't know what to do with all of it and I certainly didn't understand it.

"How did I get here?"

I sobbed hard for all of these people. Their grief overpowered me and appeared to transcend time. Even as I write this now, I vividly recall the pain. It was like being at a funeral for a hundred people, not personally knowing anyone yet feeling their sorrow and anger.

I left the tree and ran back to my house. In that moment, I realized I had come out of this dream, like when you are suddenly awakened and startled from sleep.

What did all of this mean? Oh, I'm so confused, I thought. *What do I do with these feelings I'm experiencing – they're not mine or are they? Who can I talk to about this? I don't know anyone that would even understand what I've just experienced or know how to explain this.*

I went on with my day but in a sort of stupor, as if in a state of fog.

For a while after, I didn't mention this to anyone for fear they would think I was crazy. Frankly, I felt a little like I was. Even more than that, I experienced this intense sadness, which didn't feel like mine, and yet somehow now it was.

Over the next few days, I heard a man's voice several times. Then one day I had a vision along with the voice. It was of an older Native American male. He was dressed in skins with braided hair and a beautiful large feather in a headband that he wore around his head. He had a weathered yet kind face and looked as if he was a very important person in the native culture. I felt it imperative to communicate with him.

Although I was somewhat fearful, I asked his name and he replied, *"Two Feather."* He went on to tell me, *"You have built your house on sacred land and intruded on a burial ground. Grandmother* (he was referring to the voice at the tree) *is the carrier of this information and played this in a kind of dream for you, so you will understand. There are many souls that are stuck in this between realm, after death, that are wandering and need to be freed. Would you help them cross over?"*

I was surprised to hear this but kind of relieved to at least know what had happened and why. I didn't quite understand all of this, but I knew we shouldn't have disturbed their sacred land. It made me so upset to think we had disrupted the energy here although it was clear I could help in some way.

To cross over after death means to enter a

spiritual realm before incarnating again—a space in time and reality, after a person reaches their Earthly death and their spirit leaves their physical body. This soul part that has left the body will transition to unite with its Higher Spirit self, the pure soul self-originated in Source or God.

I didn't know anything about this or how to even do it. You see, I was raised Catholic and unsure about life after death at this time in my life. I was willing to try to help them because they were wandering, lost and stuck somewhere. After all, I disturbed their resting place and needed to make this right — but I would need guidance on how to proceed.

"How am I to do this and where do I find someone that will understand?"

For a little while I didn't appear to have any more communication with Two Feather or the Grandmother tree. It felt as if I were on my own. In hindsight, I now understand I was to start my journey to explore more within this realm of helping these spirits.

I finally got up enough nerve to share this in confidence with someone who was an acquaintance and who I thought might understand. He recommended I talk with someone he knew by the name of Gene.

I discovered that Gene was a Spirit Medium, someone who communicates with deceased spirits. Gene indicated that he was familiar with those that had not crossed and therefore were left wandering. Upon reading the energy on my land, he felt the spirit of a young girl, about ten years old, who still wandered in our house after this battle. He also mentioned that there were others who were either lost or who mourned their loved ones on the land and who also needed to move on.

Even though these sad events happened about two hundred years ago, it was still very real at that moment. Time, as we know or think of it, is not linear, it all happens simultaneously—that may be very hard to wrap the mind around as the brain is trained to think in one moment following another, in a linear way.

This was all a real happening, but at another vibrational frequency, much like a radio or television station you would tune into. I had tuned into this particular vibrational happening and was in some way a part of it all.

Now, what about this young spirit girl, who even the dog had experienced in our home? As I understood it, her father and uncle had crossed over when they died, but she remained stuck in this alternate reality. Spirits often become trapped in this reality, still feeling they are alive, not comprehending that they are dead and unable to cross over. This spirit clung to our family, desperate to be connected to a family like the one she had lost.

With the help of Gene talking me through it, I was able to call upon the spirit of the father to come and meet his daughter. She wanted to be with her family. Her father's spirit and others shone so brightly that she was able to follow and cross.

I now realized this was the reason I couldn't sell my house — and why others didn't want to buy it. On some level within myself, it was beginning to make some sense, although still strange to me.

After a little time, Two Feather reached out to me after the crossing of the girl and others. He asked if I would seal the land so this would bring closure to all. He guided me to chant several phrases while pouring salt around the house and property—a wonderful closing ceremony for all and an incredible opening for me.

Within a short while afterward, Two Feather began to speak more frequently to me. He asked if I would work with other souls that were stuck and lost to help them also cross over.

As time went on, he helped me to expand on my capabilities. He began by teaching me how to read the symbology of the energy I was either feeling or seeing. When a picture or a feeling would come to me, I needed to comprehend it and know how to run it through the filters of my own mind and describe it in words. Imagine not understanding a foreign language or sign language and then attempting to translate it into something comprehensible—it's a challenging task.

I learned to become more attuned to my senses. I learned to read what the physical body conveyed to me, and also learned how to read or hear what is held in an object or a spirit's message.

Once I learned how to listen and translate, I found myself able to expand my gift. I am now able to see or hear an ailment or illness that may be undetected, then relate it to certain circumstances in a person's life. Often, I can just be in an energy field and hear or sense what it is communicating in a remote experience. Sometimes, I can place my hand on something or someone and hear or pick up information this way as well.

With becoming ill, as I mentioned earlier in this chapter, I had begun to lose some of my left-brain function and memory, which enabled me to learn to trust my intuition more. I could get out of my left-brain chatter and allow energy and spirits to speak and guide me through my senses and intuition. This ability to perceive energy or vibration happens because we are all a part of the same energy field—**consciousness.** I would compare this ability to looking up the desired information from an encyclopedia available to all of us.

This experience was like being in a new class of a different kind. It is personal to share this capability with others, and also challenging as there is so much to learn. Strangely, I felt I somehow already knew how to do this, as if I had forgotten and only just now remembered.

Most importantly, this opened up a whole new world... connected me with my gifts and capabilities... and revealed another purpose for why I'm here. Truly, this was the "end all" learning experience and yet it was only the beginning of the journey into my destiny.

Food for Thought

Have you explored your gifts?
What is your personal story?
What have you learned from it?
Have you met your guide(s)?

Chapter Two

Connecting the Dots...

Your connection to spirit is eternal
and simply needs to be fully realized ~ LW

My life is rich with lessons that consistently teach me to trust the voice within — although admittedly at times its message is not a comfortable one, nor have I always wanted to listen and follow the guidance. Below is a story about one of those challenging times when following that nudging voice was especially difficult for me.

Watching children grow from childhood through the teenage years can be a rough and challenging time for any mother. In our society, unlike indigenous cultures, we haven't instilled a "rites of passage" to help children find their identity into adulthood. At the time when my youngest son was beginning to explore who he was, I had been studying the wisdom of native cultures and wondered why we as a society don't implement more of this into our own culture. I thought, *"Ceremonies and rituals are a wonderful way to give teens the tools to learn and grow."*

This brings me to the voice within…Oh, that voice…. Sometimes, it asks us to do things we don't really want to do, but therein lies the learning. I watched my youngest son growing up and, at times, wrestling with those feelings of being a teen and becoming an adult. I have a good relationship with him, but there were questions and some guidance issues that, as a mom, I couldn't provide in his time of searching – it was outside my realm of knowledge and experience. He needed some kind of guidance at this transition point and I felt uncertain of how to approach this issue. Now you might think after raising three other children I would be clearer on this, but somehow this one was different in his needs. I recognized that it wasn't anything religious I was looking for to assist my son, but I wasn't clear what was needed.

While shopping in town one day, I wandered into a small Native American shop. As I entered, I heard the voice within say, *"this is the person."*

I thought to myself, "*What does that mean? What person?"*

When that voice speaks to me it doesn't often say much, so it's up to me to expand on what is being said. I thought, *"This is strange as I hadn't even asked a question,"* although I'm certain I did so subconsciously.

As I looked around, the shop owner stood by the front counter. I knew from a glance that he was Native American. We exchanged looks, he greeted me warmly and we both smiled. This wasn't the first time I had been in his store as it was a friendly place and I enjoyed being amidst all of the native goods, jewelry, footwear, dream catchers, photos, clothing etcetera; but I still didn't know what that voice wanted me to find. I looked around a bit more, but not understanding what the voice intended me to do, I left.

Over the next few days I felt a recurring hard nudging sense to return to the native shop. I decided to visit once again and I heard that voice say, *"this is where you'll find your answer."*

"What answer is it referring to?" I wondered.

I always have so many questions in my inquisitive mind, but what specifically was it speaking of? Was it the one about my son? What did it want me to do? I felt it was trying to help me find solutions, but how was the shop owner going to be able to help me when I didn't even know him?

I thought, *"It is difficult and uncomfortable to talk about something so personal when I don't know what to say or ask."*

Despite the uncertainty to connect what I had heard with any clear instructions; the nudging grew stronger the longer I stood there in the shop and by now wouldn't leave me alone. It's as if a child is nudging you when you don't pay attention and you finally surrender.

I answered, "Well, if I'm gonna do this, it's now or never."

I mustered enough guts and timidly approached him. I announced, "I feel kind of embarrassed for telling you this when I don't even know you. I feel I'm to talk to you about my son and ask how you can help me with him in some way?" I continued, "I have a son who's a teenager—I think he needs some kind of indigenous guidance—a kind of 'rites of passage.' I don't really completely understand this, but I'm hoping you can help me fill in the blanks, as I'm not quite sure what I'm even talking about. But, you see, I have a voice inside that speaks to me, and it's been nudging me for days now and won't leave me alone."

Ed, the shop owner, chuckled and my embarrassment grew. I thought, "*He thinks I'm crazy and I'll never be able to step into this shop again."*

Ed smiled—he had an openness to him and a kind and friendly face that eased my awkwardness. He replied, "You don't know how right you are to come and talk with me. Every week, I teach a small group of people an ancient form of martial arts combined with native wisdom."

Ed explained that he was first a student many years ago and now a teacher of this great art. He remarked, "Why don't you bring your son down to a meeting and we can see if it would be a good fit for him? I don't ask many people into this group but somehow it seems right."

I thanked him for understanding and set off home to share the news with my son. I was excited and relieved this came together the way it did, and happy I followed the guidance. It amazed me how intently the guide behind the internal voice listened—"*Be careful what you ask for,*" I thought.

This spirit brought what was needed, although I hadn't known what or where to find it on my own. We all have intuition guided by spirits, but at this time in my learning, I didn't understand how many spirits were working with me.

I often say, "I believe we are in charge of our intentions and desires, but not the scenery or the way the message is delivered." In other words, who will bring the message or information or how it will look is all a part of the process of co-creating. It's a beautiful thing when we allow the creating to unfold. I also feel I couldn't do it better myself as I would probably mess it up left to my own thinking.

This all felt so right to me. I truly hoped my son would want to connect and that Ed and this group would help him transition into this new phase of life. The teaching of this old tradition brought about a sense of honor, encouragement and community for him. He learned how to better trust himself—his sense of awareness deepened as did his trust in that voice within of spiritual guidance. He expanded his passion and learned about the subtle sense of energy. Afterward, I knew this was exactly what he needed and appreciated how beautifully it all came together.

As for me, I watched my son grow in his own wisdom, power and sense of belonging within an understanding community. It was heartwarming to know that he received the kind of guidance I would not have been able to provide at that time on my own. He received his much needed 'rite of passage' and at exactly the right time. Through such experiences in my life, I have learned the value of trusting that this guidance comes from within and that all the help we need is available to us. Admittedly, sometimes, the lessons are difficult when we can't understand it all—but that's where *trusting* becomes essential.

Participating in this group was one of the best times in my son's life, and he draws upon those teachings to this day. This is a perfect example of one of those notable milestones that you want to write about in your child's baby book.

I continue to learn to trust that inner voice – and urge you to do the same. It has your best interest and highest intentions at heart—spirit will never steer you wrong. Although we can't always connect all of the dots on our own, stepping in with faith and trust in this process is the key to obtaining the answers we need.

All of us have undermining beliefs that we carry from lifetime to lifetime or formulate in our younger years that help to paint our future. Those who have survived their childhood (I say jokingly) have enough information about life to get them through the rest of their days.

The next story is a great unfolding of the way the spirits and our own Higher Self assist us to adjust our beliefs or what I'll call our illusions in order to evolve.

Here is what Bruce Lipton, Ph.D., a cellular biologist has to say about beliefs: "Perception is awareness shaped by belief. Beliefs 'control' perception. Rewrite beliefs and you rewrite perception. Rewrite perception and you rewrite genes and behavior...I am free to change how I respond to the world, so as I change the way I see the world, I change my genetic expression. We are not victims of our genes. We are masters of our genetics."

Many years ago, I had a friend named Jessie, who at the time was a fifty-nine-year-old woman experiencing heart pain and headaches that intensified whenever the holiday season approached. She had experienced these symptoms for many years, but *only* at this specific time of the year. Jessie had previously undergone a stress test for the heart and an MRI for her migraines, but with no resulting evidence of any unusual health problems. When a diagnosis eluded her, she became frustrated. Jessie simply thought it was due to trying to get everything done over the holidays, as many of us experience, but still it perplexed her.

One day when we were having a talk together in my office, she mentioned to me, "You know I'm really not looking forward to the holidays this year."

I asked, "Why? Is it all the commercialism that takes away from the spirit of the season?"

She replied, "No, that's not it at all. I can't really put my finger on it, but the same thing happens to me every year, I don't really understand it."

I asked, "Would you like to have a session? We might be able to unlock the mystery of what is happening. It usually begins to open us to what is hidden deep within."

She agreed and we set up her appointment in the days following. Upon scanning her body's energy for information and reading the symbology, I discovered this was connected to a Christmas from when she was a young child. Jessie was unaware of holding sadness in her heart for so many years. It appeared as if she had buried it away so deep that she hadn't even remembered this particular event.

During Christmas Eve when she was twelve years old, Jessie's parents had been invited out to a party. As they left early that evening and said goodbye, Jessie noticed her parents hadn't put up any ornaments or a tree before leaving. She really never knew whether they had intended to decorate when they returned. From her perspective, both she and her brother were left alone while their parents went out to have fun. Jessie, at this time in her life, knew there was no Santa Claus, but her brother who was only six years old still believed in his existence.

"This is awful," she thought. *"This will absolutely ruin my brother's Christmas. He will for sure no longer believe in Santa Claus and*

everything will be ruined." Jessie loved her brother and certainly didn't want to see him hurt.

The responsibility to prepare the home for Christmas was quite a burden for a twelve-year-old. She needed to get her brother to bed, decorate, trim the tree, and set up the presents for him—oh, and don't forget the cookies! At her young age, Jessie's belief was that her parents should have stayed home to do all of this. She was too young to carry this burden and was left feeling quite angry.

Jessie held this emotion in her heart and in her subconscious for forty-seven years. While I scanned and asked for healing from the spirits I work with, I saw a white dove float down from the heavens, bringing a sprig of holly and placing it inside her heart.

My deep sense and understanding of the

symbology was this: Holly is a plant we associate with the Christmas season. If you've ever tried to pick a branch, most likely you discovered how prickly it can be. I associated it as guarding her heart issues, like a fortress. Guarding of the heart along with the headaches meant Jessie still carried some anger and resentment at this time of year toward her parents (even though they were now both deceased). Inside, she suffered this pain and closed off her heart during the holiday season, protecting the pain she has carried for so many years.

The white dove descending from the heavens symbolized a pure message from a higher place—Source or maybe what you call God—a dove carrying a symbol of peace, love and healing for this Christmas season. I knew this dove was bringing an opportunity for her to heal her past and a greater feeling of love in the season.

The language of these messages and visions is that of symbology, which enables one to understand the information and then convey the message to the person. Most of the time, this becomes obvious within a session but not always. This is why it's imperative to learn your own dictionary of symbology because each person's is different.

After the session and during that present Christmas season, holly kept showing up for Jessie in several forms. She hadn't told anyone about her experience with me, so the following events came as quite a surprise to her— especially because she hadn't held any attachment to holly until prior to that session. One day her husband came home from work bearing a beautiful holly bush for her to plant outside. He wasn't the kind that brought gifts, so this was quite unusual. Then on Christmas morning, her daughter gave her a beautiful small charm bracelet but with only one charm on it. You guessed it: it was a piece of holly.

Jessie was amazed at how this was all unfolding in her life.

She told me after, "I feel that somehow my parents are acknowledging what happened and how I felt about that Christmas. I now feel quite a sense of forgiveness within, like a burden has been lifted. These signs truly were healing to me."

In the years that followed, Jessie never again had heart pain along with a headache during the Christmas season.

The dots within our lives truly do connect even when we don't see how or why. It can reveal through an "aha" moment that strikes us unexpectedly. It can also be as large and obvious as a billboard because we haven't been listening to the small subtle voice until it sometimes declares itself dramatically. And then at other times it is a person or something you read that speaks to us to trigger a thought and sets off a chain reaction. The dots work in subtle ways and can feel like a difficult puzzle of a thousand pieces when all of it isn't revealed at once, as in the story of Hansel and Gretel, leaving breadcrumbs along the path to show the way. Trust that the answers are there for us—our intention drives life to happen. Developing our understanding of how life and spirit communicate to us can be a challenge and yet it's all synchronistic. Eventually everything connects – people, ideas, objects etcetera. The quality of the connection is the key to such communication.

We don't really know what the picture will reveal...until we connect the dots

Food for thought

How do you recognize and connect your dots?

Can you interpret your visions or dreams?

Do you have a personal dictionary of symbology?

How you do receive your intuition?

Which of your senses do you use most?

Chapter Three

Is it emotion or intuition?

Seek your own voice and vision, rather than adopting someone else's

I've learned over the many years as my intuition and guidance has been developing that when I feel an uncomfortable emotion—one I don't want to feel—I am reminded, "go inside and look deeper." If I look hard enough, sometimes needing to wait for answers that are unknown yet to be revealed, the truth will become clearly known. It's about looking at something and not hiding from it, which results in us pushing it farther away, but instead squaring off with it – turning and facing it – not avoiding or running from it. This is how we get to the core and understand ourselves.

Now, when I feel an uncomfortable emotion; I ask myself, "*What is it that is really going on? Is it an emotion or intuition?*"

On my path of self-discovery, I've wanted to know more – more about myself, more of who I really am, about what makes me tick, and more about why I'm here. I've also heard others share these same questions… unable to answer them.

In earlier years I didn't always feel this way. It isn't easy to look at yourself objectively and truthfully. I now want to honestly know what I'm feeling, the circumstance and why. I go deeper within through my journey work, open up the energy and look for what the root cause is – asking for more to be revealed and then how to adjust or heal it.

If I don't take the time to understand myself and the world, if I suppress what I'm experiencing—I don't use the opportunity of lessons to expand my awareness.

No experience is ever wasted because each contains a lesson. Maybe this might be too much for some folks, looking inside often, learning through direct experiences to fulfill the mission of our lives. When we actually feel the experience, then the deeper we feel it and the more anchored it is for us in a profound way.

We are not physical beings having a spiritual experience. We are spiritual beings, having a physical experience.

Put in these terms, the challenges are all a

part of the Earth curriculum. Daily life is my classroom, each lesson is my homework. Lessons reappear until we master them and create a learning experience for the next step on our journey.

Several years ago, as I was doing some shamanic journey work one morning, I found myself in a very deep hypnotic state when I accessed some information. This was quite significant and intriguing to me, and as the experience unfolded, I said to myself, "I couldn't possibly be making this up in my imagination as I don't have any information regarding this era."

When these experiences occur, I also find that they are completely validating for this reason. After this journey occurred, I researched what I saw further for my curiosity. I needed to know in what period of time it took place, who the people were, and why it happened. The clothing and manner in which people were dressed helped to divulge further information.

The scene was of the Moorish period of time, back in the 700's AD. This time refers to the rule of the Moors in the Iberian Peninsula which began in 711 and continued in one way or the other until 1492. This period began when Moorish military leader Tariq Bin Ziyad crossed the Strait of Gibraltar and defeated a significant Visigothic army in 711.

I was suddenly in the forest, it was dark, probably early morning before dawn. I suddenly found myself in a scene on horseback and right in the middle of a battle – It was extremely explicit, feeling as if I were right there. Suddenly, a man on a horse charged in on me. I turned and lunged a sword into his chest. Blood spewed everywhere. My adrenaline pumped so hard that I thought my heart would jump out of my body.

Even the horse snorted and sweated with fear. As I watched this person fall off his horse and onto the ground – dead – I was mortified. I had just killed someone. How could I do this? In my brain I couldn't quite understand it, this felt so foreign to me! I looked around while others continued to battle. There was a lot of noise, screaming and blood everywhere!

In that life, what I understood to be considered a victorious experience was not. It was quite the opposite. It was one of the most horrible experiences within myself I had ever felt. The person I am today has a difficult time squishing spiders and can never consciously think of hurting anything or anyone.

In that moment deep in my hypnotic state where I experienced this other life, I realized I was to stop the killing. No more war. It doesn't solve anything to hurt anyone or anything. This was a breakthrough understanding of that period of time for me, the reason this spontaneous past life came to me. I am who I am today due to that realization of that lifetime —a turning point for the sake of the soul's growth and the collective good. This conviction ran deep and was integral in my soul's journey.

We all have experienced lives where we have been the victim and the victimizer, a part of the dark side. This duality is part of the Divine Grand Plan designed for the soul's evolution. By navigating through the darkness, the soul seeks to realize peace and love.

Is it Emotion or is it an Intuitive Moment?

Whether it is emotion or intuition, there

is something to be learned. It's difficult to always discern between these two aspects within a person. Ask yourself, "Where does this come from?" Give yourself a moment to listen for the answer – it's important to hear the internal response – you might be surprised; discernment is key.

If it's emotion, be honest with yourself. This is a hard one. We sometimes don't want to be completely truthful with ourselves—at times we prefer avoidance (taking the easy road) and don't want to be accountable. Face it – take responsibility for who you are. It's you – it's ok, there is no such thing as perfect. Learn something – be accountable - grow. This is who you are—accept, understand, and modify. You may need to wrestle awhile until you can accept what you uncover. Every day is a blank canvas. We all know that our deep emotions take time to adjust and heal. This is why we reincarnate over and over — to learn until we get it. Wisdom isn't born overnight.

Now, if its intuition...ahhh...again pay attention! There's a gift in this for you from your helpers, guides, teachers or Higher Self ... they're calling to you. There is much learning here in the classroom of Earth school. At any given moment you are either the student or teacher — can you look and see through both pairs of glasses?

The following is a little, but powerful, story—one that exemplifies these points. It is one I'll never forget and that continues to teach me.

My husband, Bob, and I planned a few days of summer fun one long August weekend. Through the internet, Bob had set up a tour to visit one of the mysterious energy vortexes (vortices). A very powerful energy is said to emanate from the red rocks in Sedona, Arizona.

A vortex is thought to be a swirling center of energy that are conducive to healing, meditation and self-exploration. This area in Arizona is known to be especially alive with this energy and reputed to create great inspiration that leaves you recharged and uplifted. Since we are both very adventurous and neither had ever been there, we were very excited to go.

I had been especially sensitive to energy for many years and looked forward to working with my clair senses. In much the same way that we use our five physical senses for seeing, hearing, touching, tasting and smelling, we all also have the potential to experience psychic sensitivity corresponding to the sense.

Clairvoyance: clear vision - to visually perceive "within the mind's eye", receiving extra sensory impressions, and symbols in the form of "inner sight" or mental images which are perceived without the aid of the physical eyes and beyond the limitations of ordinary time and space - something existing in that real, A clairvoyant is one who receives extrasensory impressions, and symbols in the form of "inner sight" or mental images which are perceived without the aid of the physical eyes and beyond the limitations of ordinary time and space.

Clairaudience: clear audio/hearing – to perceive sounds or words and extrasensory noise, from sources, broadcast from spiritual or ethereal realm in the form of "inner ear" or mental tone, which are perceived without the aid of the physical ear.

Clairsentience: clear sensation or feeling – to perceive information by a "feeling" within the whole body, without any outer stimuli related to the feeling or information.

Clairalience: clear smelling – to smell a fragrance/odor of substance or food which is not in one's surroundings. These odors are perceived without the aide of the physical nose.

Clairkinesthesia: clear physically touching/sensing – more commonly known as psychometry. To handle an object or touch an area and perceive through the palms of one's hands information about the article or its owner, or history that was not previously known by the person.

Claircognizance: clear knowing – the ability to know something without really knowing how you know it. Think about something such as a question and receive answers internally within the mind.

We arrived at the office of the company that was to take us out early Friday morning, excited and prepared for this energy adventure.

It was already warm early this morning and we knew it was going to be hot in the desert — little did we know how "hot" it would really get that day.

Now, I just want to mention at this point that we had already paid in advance for this very pricey tour – some things you just have to do... Upon walking into the office, we sat down at the guide's desk, noting his name was Carl. Within five minutes of him mapping out "the three-hour tour," there was a very loud crash. Several ceiling tiles fell down in front of our chairs on top of his desk! If it is true and there are no accidents, I took this as a sign to expect the unexpected. I won't say "to expect the worst", as that's a matter of perspective. This was to be an impactful learning for both Bob and I, although, regarding whatever was to happen, I wasn't getting a good vibe! Nevertheless, shortly after listening to

Carl—even though my feelings weren't exactly warm and fuzzy—I decided to give it a go anyway, a sort of benefit of the doubt. Now as hindsight is 20/20, I usually rethink such thoughts.

As Carl stepped into the jeep, I walked around the other side to get in– along with Bob. I whispered in Bob's ear, "Do we really need to do this tour with him? I don't have a good vibe."

Bob replied, "Well, we did pay already so we should see what this is all about."

I must admit I felt a bit hesitant to continue, but I went along the way not wanting to rock the boat. I listened to what Carl said, taking it all in because I didn't really know much about the area, and relied on him to guide us. I began noticing how Carl would speak primarily to Bob rather than addressing both of us. I figured he simply connected better with men than women and shrugged it off.

As we began our trek into the desert, very shortly after walking along the trail, Carl exclaimed, "Watch out there's a vortex, stand back!" Then a few moments later, again "There's another one!"

I'll admit I didn't see or feel anything at this point, but I'm not sure I was actually expecting to with this type of energy. Anyhow, we were careful to watch our steps along the way.

After another ten minutes Carl shouted, "There's another vortex!"

I began to wonder what this guy was talking about because I was not feeling these vibes. In any case, we walked along for a bit longer and he shouts again, "Shaaa, there's another one!"

By now, I started thinking that Carl didn't know what he was talking about for a few reasons. One, I wasn't connecting to what he was saying. And, two, I didn't think that a vortex experience would be this way, although I remained open minded.

I began feeling taken advantage of – which then made me angry. I thought, *"This guy took our money and I wasn't getting the kind of experience I thought this to be."*

Another few minutes went by and he exclaims, "There's another one – another vortex. Don't you see it?"

Well, I had had about enough at this point and said to Carl, "I think we'd like to end this excursion and we'd like our money returned to us."

He replied, "No, that's not possible at this time because there are no refunds once you've paid, therefore you might as well finish the trip".

By this point, our excursion had

progressed for about an hour. I tried to pull my husband aside, although it was difficult because Carl refused to leave his side.

"This guy definitely has some problems," I thought.

I said to Bob, "I really don't believe he knows what he's talking about and think we should cut our losses and end the trip, I think he's crazy and I don't trust him."

Bob replied, "Let's just stick it out as we're paid in full, we might experience something soon."

Knowing my husband as I do, I figured he would say this because he's a peace maker and never likes to ruffle feathers. Besides, he really thought we might still get an experience. I decided to give it a bit more time, bite my tongue and go along with it.

As you can imagine, this continued to go

on for a bit longer and, as my anger intensified, I wanted to put an end to his nonsense.

Simultaneously, Carl decided to make this journey easier on himself by trying to separate my husband from me. He said to Bob, "Why don't you come with me and Laurie you go that way and we'll meet up at the end in about an hour?"

I truly think he had had enough of me and my comments. By now, I didn't know where we were or how to get back to the road because he had taken us off the path. I was really angry!

Carl then said, "The trip must go on" .... *so he thought!*...

We went only about twenty steps further—I was extremely hot and very tired by now – and feeling incredibly drained. So, I found a great spot to rest under a tree in the shade, which is not one of those abundant happenings in the desert. As I leaned up against this tree, ready to quit this madness, I heard a woman's voice.

The voice said in a kind and calm tone but with authority, much like a wise grandmother might sound, *"Are you going to let him take your power?"*

I wasn't completely certain but felt this wasn't my mind speaking. I knew it was coming from somewhere else, but where?

I wondered, *"What am I hearing and where out here is this coming from?"*

I waited and listened, but that is all the voice said to me.

After a moment, I thought, *"This is a wise spirit guiding me again."*

I began to really think about what she had said as I rested a few more minutes. I thought, *"She's right, why get angry? It's not going to solve anything?"*

I was angry when I believed I didn't have a choice, until I realized I ***did*** have a choice. The choice not to be angry from this point, to change the circumstance, and take action for what I thought best. Finally, I realized that the angrier I became, the more I surrendered my power as well as my ability to reason and act clearly—anger wasn't solving anything.

I left the shade of the tree and walked a few more feet away. Then, I turned to my husband and said, "I'm choosing to be finished with this and to find my way back to the road – do you want to come along with me?"

I'll admit, at this moment, this was a hard decision. I didn't want to ruffle feathers between my husband and myself. I really wanted him to come with me, but however it turned out, I was done with all of this madness and had made my decision.

Bob thought for a moment and said, "I agree, I'm done too, let's go back". We then turned to Carl and said, "We are finished, this is where we part ways!"

And we left, without any refund, although it really didn't matter at that point.

It took a while to find our way out because we had veered off the path. Fortunately, we had great guidance and Bob has a good sense of direction. We made it back, very parched but safe.

It was a powerful lesson for me to learn about anger, choice, and my power. Power didn't come through anger, but through being able to make a clear choice and acting on it. I didn't need to be angry, clearly that wasn't helping the situation. My power rested in the freedom to make choices based on what I deemed best in the moment. Choosing and speaking from a balanced state actually enhanced my power.

The wise Grandmother voice was what I needed exactly at that moment. She made me aware that I am empowered by keeping my cool and making the choice that was right for me. I will never forget those sweet words. I often refer back to this experience when I realize I am getting angry, then realizing I'm losing my power.

As I've listened to my guidance for many years now, I've never experienced these wonderful spirits *tell* me what to do, they *guide*. I always have free will to choose. This is what being in our Earthly school is all about. It was clear that choosing to listen helped me make the wisest of decisions.

The word "guide" is clearly the best way to describe the profound help we all have.

Guide; noun, a person who advises or shows the way to others.

Great guidance comes to those who listen....

Food for Thought

When do you listen to your mind? To your inner voice?

What situations allow you to lose your power?

Can you remember a time when an experience taught you a life lesson?

Chapter Four
The Sixteen Mile Short Cut

"The Pessimist Sees Difficulty in
Every Opportunity.
The Optimist Sees Opportunity in
Every Difficulty."
– Winston Churchill

The Wolves Within – A Cherokee Indian Legend

A wise old Grandfather said to his

grandson, who came to him with anger at a friend who had done him an injustice, "Let me tell you a story. I too, at times, have felt a great hate for those that have taken so much with no sorrow for what they do. But hate wears you down and does not hurt your enemy. It is like taking poison and wishing your enemy would die. I have struggled with these feelings many times." He continued, "It is as if there are two wolves inside me. One is good and does no harm. He lives in harmony with all around him and does not take offense when no offense was intended. He will only fight when it is right to do so, and in the right way. The other wolf, ah! He is full of anger. The littlest thing will set him into a fit of temper. He fights everyone, all the time, for no reason. He cannot think because his anger and hate are so great. It is helpless anger, for his anger will change nothing. Sometimes, it is hard to live with these two wolves inside me, for both of them try to dominate my spirit."

The boy looked intently into his Grandfather's eyes and asked, "Which one wins, Grandfather?"

The Grandfather smiled and quietly said, "The one I feed."

Which one do you feed?

A.) There is wisdom all around, even in the times when we don't think or see it – we only have to pay attention.

B.) There is no right or wrong, if we don't succeed at either finishing or achieving our purpose – we'll return to learn again.

C.) There is no one standing over us telling us what we *must* learn or *how* to do it. It's up to us with whom and how we evolve. The choices we make determine our Karma.

You've heard the word Karma, but what does it mean? Karma is a **conscious and intentional action** that decides the fate of the future for a person.

So, for example, if you make fun of Sally often enough to cause her to hold onto being upset, in turn she starts to bully others, and now you have created Karma. It's incredible, the ripple effect that we're a part of so being conscious of our actions and deeds is critical. You will have to come back to right the wrongs you intentionally produce.

I'm told, "hold a thought for seventeen seconds and the law of attraction kicks in. Hold a thought for sixty-eight seconds and manifestation has begun."

The Power of Choice is Yours...Every Choice Leads to Wisdom

In this next story, our collective choice provided a rich adventure on the river. I've had many experiences which have taught me that life ebbs and flows—and the best option is to *go with the flow.*

Resistance isn't always pleasant nor the most comfortable path to take. We can either take the sixteen-mile short cut (this being the long hard road) or the easier road. Now, sometimes life chooses for you, but when you can make the choice – go with the flow.

Water is a great teacher of many things, the one I find most helpful is "flow".

Consider - *To flow; verb, move along or go continuously in a current or stream from one place to another.*

Oh, no! Not Another Learning Experience!

When my children were in their early twenties, we all wanted to go white-water rafting. White-water refers to the whitecaps you see as water flows along. Sometimes it can be rough, and sometimes mild.

One summer afternoon, while living in southern Maine, we rounded up a few friends, along with our family – nine in all— and set off on our rafting adventure. We drove from Maine up to North Conway, New Hampshire, about two hours north of us, where the river runs downward from the mountaintop. This is an area that remains snow-capped year-round and oh, it is very cold, to say the least.

We chose to go on the morning trip, which meant getting up at the crack of dawn and heading out. As morning began to break, the sun barely peeked out of the clouds, and it looked to be more cloudy than sunny that day.

It was as much an expedition to get to the "put in sight" for the rafts as it was for the trip down river. It was a picturesque drive and it was a fun road trip up the mountain.

After arriving and sitting for a short movie that explained all the details to observe for safety requirements, we all loaded into the raft. Where you sit in the raft determines a position for paddling that you will take during the expedition, which I didn't realize at the time.

My husband, Bob, and I sat in the back, at the end of the raft. My brother was in the middle, and our friend Pat was at the helm. If you knew Pat, you would figure him to be up in front steering the boat—he was a take-charge kind of guy. The rest were along the sides of the raft, all of us with paddles in hand and ready for an adventure. In the back on the edge of the raft sat our instructor. He was quite a character with a dry sense of humor, knick-named "the Fonz."

There were other rafts along the trip, about eight or more within view. Sometimes we were very close to another raft—you could reach out and touch them.

We started out on the river nice and slow, easing on down. As we flowed along, about five minutes into it all, Pat, who was up front, asked the Fonz, "Hey there's some rough waters ahead, how should we handle it?"

Fonz replied, "Well, there are two ways to look at this. You can have the slow and easy way, or you can experience all the river has to offer you! What do you want to do?"

Within a moment, we all simultaneously shouted, "Let's go for it!"

Fonz shouted, "Get ready to paddle, listen to what I say—paddle right to go left and left to go right, paddle hard as you can and I'll tell you when to paddle opposite – it's gonna be hard and fast, but the most fun you can have!"

Anyone who has ever been white-water rafting knows that the river is unpredictable because there are twists, turns and squalls. A squall in the river is a brief but intense motion of water either twirling or furiously flowing.

Well, it was all of that and more. We worked together as a great team effort to actually go into or flow with the squall, which turns you up and down and all around, bumping you all over the water. It was very intense, to say the least, but absolutely fantastically fun.

When we came through it, we were all laughing, screaming, soaking wet, and checking that we were all still in the raft. What a fantastic experience it was! So much so, that the rafts back end—where Bob, I, and the Fonz were sitting—had been completely engulfed with water. This was also documented by the fact that there were cameras set up along the river to catch photos as we went on by. We actually made the front cover of their publication that year! It was an amazing picture to see and visual proof that we truly experienced the most the river had to offer.

From that point on, we hit a few more intense squalls and knew exactly how to handle them. It was thrilling and worth every moment.

This memory will forever remain etched in my mind for a few reasons. First, making memories with people that you love to be with is *priceless*.

Second, I learned a great lesson that day on the river. Some days we don't feel like struggling and some days we have more stamina. There's no judgement from anyone in how or what you choose – it's up to each of us. We're in charge of how we arrive.

That day, the river gave me a perfect perspective of the flow of life for which I will always be grateful. Sometimes it's rough and difficult, and sometimes it's calm and easy. We were faced with a choice—resist or flow.

Going with the flow gave me the best experience—I wanted the most out of it and got it. Life is always filled with this movement, whichever way you choose to flow – and it's all a learning experience.

On a deeper level, we as individual souls - all have the same goal: to evolve, fueled by the desire to progress in wisdom. We make a plan, a contract, before reincarnating. In brief, at the time before each incarnation, when we are of our pure soul form, we determine what we will look like, who we want to do this next incarnation with, and in what type of setting or situation to do it.

As an analogy, if you have ever played the game "Clue", a detective game to solve who done it, with what, and where - it was Professor Peacock who did it in the library with the candlestick. Sometimes souls will progress in their mission and sometimes not. Sometimes we can exceed what we actually plan – again it's our choice.

Adversity is one way the universe gets our attention. Physical pain talks to us sometimes more often than emotionally. In the emotional imbalance, is where our illusions and resistance exist. Pain is inevitable, but when we learn to listen, and choose not to resist, the suffering dissolves and our path opens up wide.

Whichever type of soul you are, learning to ride the human challenges or limitations, serves to expand the human and universal consciousness – doing it together and supporting each other as we go along.

Food for Thought

In life, do you go with the flow or resist?

Do you pay attention to the subtleties or do you need a billboard?

Do you find the wisdom in your choices?

Chapter Five

What Pair of Glasses Do You Wear?

Begin each day as if it is on purpose

Focus....I think this is an interesting concept. What comes to mind is putting on a pair of glasses to see better. I had a realization of this when I reached the wonderful age of fifty-five and went to the eye doctor for glasses. It was amazing how much better I could see with those glasses.

Something else that becomes apparent

when I think of the word focus is keeping my eye on the ball. When something isn't in our focus, we can become clouded by other intrusions and it's easy to lose our objective, to lose sight of our purpose. Ultimately, we're here to find and fulfill our purpose.

Focus is a central thought that aims you in a direction, and this direction then guides you in fulfilling your purpose. It helps you get up in the morning, be prepared for the day, and stay on task. Focus helps guide our life decisions, influences behaviors, shapes goals, and creates meaning for life – I like to say, "purpose is the juice that drives you each day – the meaning to live!" Let's face it, we need to stay focused.

With life as busy as it is these days, we all do things to help us stay on task in order to meet our objective. I know I have many post-it stickies all over my office to help me stay on my path toward what I need and choose to do. Without them, I would be lost because I can get scattered and lose my sense of direction. As a homeopathic practitioner for over twenty-five years, I know that a lack of focus truly accounts for some of life's difficulties based on what many people have shared with me.

Let me bring this more into focus for you...

We all have a hand-picked, orchestrated destiny. It's a contract that every soul makes before entering embodiment. We make a plan, with the help of our Master Spirit Guide, our Higher Self, and a council of spirits specifically assigned to each soul since the beginning. This plan or contract we make is why we are here right now. As I've mentioned before, we plan who we want to learn with, how we want to do it, and in what circumstance(s), as well as what we will learn along the way. Now, it is easy to get sidetracked on Earth because there are many desires and opportunities that take us away from our goal or purpose.

This is where keeping your eye on the ball and listening to your inner guidance is necessary and helpful. If we somehow have difficulty awakening to know our path and destiny, then something will nudge once, twice and become stronger until we realign with our original intent. Do you ever get an inner feeling that won't leave you alone?

When we're not listening or not wanting to pay attention, life circumstances can come by way of an illness, trauma, or some happening that will create an experience or opportunity to redirect and refocus us on our life's purpose. I use the word opportunity as we have free will and choice, so not always do we choose to redirect ourselves. Many times, it's not at all what we're expecting, as it was for me when it was time for the game to change. There is a purpose to all of this – we are all a part of the Grand Divine Plan.

Let me elaborate on the concept of fulfilling the contract and being a part of the Grand Divine Plan. Your soul makes a decision about what it wants to learn—with the help of your Higher Self, Master Spirit Guide and your council. This includes whom you will do this with, how you will learn what you have come here to learn, and where in the cosmos you will fulfill this. This means your soul will have options of how you can learn the objective.

Allow me to elaborate further about our soul and its connections. Our soul consciousness is holographic, the light which is Source that produces an image with patterns and perspectives within it. We are both individual aspects of Source, and full holographic representations of it, all at the same time. Don't think too hard on this one because it can be confusing—simply be open to the information. If you can think in terms of a beach, each grain of sand is its own and yet a total of the entire beach. However, this does not mean that the soul individually is, in itself, an illusion. The principle of the hologram is that the part contains the whole, and yet is clearly distinguishable from it.

The primary aim of Source is to diversify into all the billions of holographic soul aspects of itself that operate in the various realms throughout the universe, in order to experience all that is and can be. So, as individualized aspects of Source who have chosen to reincarnate on this planet or elsewhere, we are merely fulfilling a small part of that objective by gaining a balance and experiences from different perspectives.

Now, the soul begins with a prenatal contract. It figures the amount of consciousness needed to get through its objective and accomplish its purpose. It's all done within a calculated concept and may be done through parallel aspects of your soul. Let's say your soul needs eight hundred years to accomplish what you wish to do, although living on Earth each life average is about eighty years. No worries, there are options.

Younger souls may decide to incarnate one life at a time. This will be enough for a younger soul's evolution as such souls are beginning to learn. Think about when a young child learns to walk. You can't run before you walk, if so, you will fall down. It took many times before you mastered this and were balanced. We need to experience falling, however many times necessary, before getting our legs firmly beneath us and developing the confidence to set out on our path.

As an older soul, before reincarnating, you know how many times we may decide we want to reach enlightenment or ascension sooner than later, although there is no race to the finish line, as there is no time limit to learning. Before you begin your soul's embodiment as an older soul, from the level of your soul between reincarnations, you know how many times you will need to accomplish your objective. It's very mathematically predictable. We are able to split and incarnate into different people or beings and in different places to accomplish our purpose.

Here's an example of how it might be for an older soul. So, my consciousness may want to spend some time on Earth, let's say four hundred years to complete my purpose. My soul can split into several people and be in different places on Earth simultaneously. I can decide how I choose to do this. I may also decide to split my consciousness into different aspects on other planets or in other realms for four hundred years. Either all at once, or as many times as I choose. Again, I will need eight hundred years in all. A soul that has gained much wisdom now can learn its objectives quicker than one life at a time. This is because it has gained more wisdom and knowledge than a younger soul.

What happens within the life of a soul is complex, as the soul doesn't always remain as a whole. As I explained, it has the opportunity to splinter or fragment, always with the objective to learn. Though sometimes the soul can fragment due to trauma, either through an accident, undergoing a serious operation or with the loss of a special person. This happens in order for that part of the soul to protect itself. In shamanic terms, soul loss is a common cause of illness. When the missing part is retrieved or decides to re-establish itself, the soul wound heals. Some part always remains in the spirit realm which is our Higher Self and is always connected to all consciousness. As we learn from these different perspectives, we evolve into the nature of our magnificent self.

If you are of the understanding that we are a part of everything, we communicate between invisible realms, which co-exist in our reality and transfer information to each of us on multi-dimensional levels through energetic cords. Some of this information is received through intuition or guidance and some as visions or perceptions, while some enter into our subconscious through the dream state.

We then process such information

through the filters of our mind and in turn redirect the associated energy out through the projection of our thoughts in order to co-create a certain reality. Simultaneously, we are transferring our thoughts back into the invisible realms, thus continuously co-creating current reality and adding experience of those with whom you are creating.

Within in this, all of existence is vibrational energy interacting and exchanging information energetically back and forth from one realm to another.

I've mentioned over time to many people, "I knew my husband before I met him." I could feel his energy about two years before I ever met him in physical form. This above mentioned is an example. I knew what I wanted in my life, the vibration went out and co-created the happening. With free will, choosing what we want or what we think about or what we intend, we vibrationally put the energy out. Of course, we are not completely aware, nor do we understand all of life's situations. So, the more energy behind thoughts, the more they are able to manifest our reality.

The following tells a little about when I was young girl and being guided to my purpose. And again, when I grew older, having the vision to keep me on my path to fulfill what I came here to accomplish. Now, clearly, at the age of five, I did not have the understanding I have now; but in some way, what I describe below helped me to stay on track and to fulfill my soulful contract.

Lying in bed at the young age of five years old, I remember speaking to a guide of mine quite often at the time (although I knew the spirit as God), I said, "I don't want to be here, this is so hard. I want to go home." Somewhere within my young mind, I knew I didn't want to do this life anymore, because it was difficult.

The return response was, "you have something that you've come to do and that your soul wants to accomplish – this is your destiny."

It wasn't the response I was looking for. I remember being upset and not understanding why. It took me many years before I could begin to understand that information. I was born with quite a strong-will and a good sense of direction in life, in other words, I knew what I wanted, and I went after it.

This strong-will kept me out of trouble and on my path of purpose. When I was twenty years old, I had a vision. It was of a baby bassinet with four heads inside. The first at the top had a pink little bonnet on its head. The next two didn't have any. Then there was a divider, a sort of small blanket and a fourth head. I was told I would have four children, the first was a girl and the rest were boys. There was a divider between the third and last baby as there was going to be a span of time unlike the others which were to be born close in age.

I can now say I have four children, the first a girl and the two following were boys. The first three were born in three and half years of each other. The fourth came four years after the third child. My focus was to have these four children and to support and love them while they do their work. They were meant to be in this world to achieve their soul's purpose with me as their mother while, at the same time, teaching me what I was meant to learn.

From a young age, I knew that this was what I was meant to do, I felt the conviction deep within. I married at a very young age, waited a few years and began having children. My first child came five years after I married. I knew I was to have this baby, in fact, I felt her deep within before she was born — I knew her before I met her. I felt a longing to be with my first child, as I now know I had been many times before and she would teach me, and I would teach her.

As much as I was to bring her into this world, I found it hard to get pregnant, I thought, *"Perhaps I am trying too hard, why isn't it happening? I had had a vision, or did I just imagine it?"*

Many people said, "Wait awhile, you're young, you have time."

I knew that having this baby was meant to be here in a serendipitous time, so I didn't give up. Timing is everything!

Finally, at the right moment, she was born. This little soul was gifted to me. I was to love her, support her, and share what I know with her. Then the next one was born, and the next and finally the last was born. It was a busy life but just right for me. I enjoyed being a mother of these wonderful children. I knew I was living the life I was meant to, and it felt right. This was my purpose for this period of my life. It was satisfying and fulfilling. I kept on my path and followed my main focus, doing the best job I knew how and helping my children grow. Though, at the time I hadn't awakened spiritually, I somehow felt guided. That's all my focus was at the time.

In the following years, as my children grew up, my purpose changed. I continued to be with my children, but now my world evolved into something new. It became time for another aspect of who I am to become clear and manifest. It was a turning point – a game changer. My path has always continued to answer the question for me, *why am I here?*

I have found that one of the underlying threads in both working in my practice or talking with people is that many have difficulty in finding the answer to this burning question— and they are looking everywhere for their answers.

I can relate to this because before I learned how to listen to guidance and the experiences I have had, I too searched outside of myself for answers. Although some search within themselves, many have difficulty hearing their guidance. This creates difficulty in knowing and answering, *Am I on the right path? Am I in the right job? Am I in the right relationship? Etcetera...*

I have spoken to many people who believe their purpose is defined by what they do for work or career. Often times, work gives us a

Laurie D. Wheeler

societal identity, such as a nurse, teacher, social worker, etcetera.

I believe our purpose isn't always what our career or work is. It can be completely different. It would appear these aspects of our identity are of an important purpose. Although, as I've heard through many of my client sessions either in homeopathic case taking, energy work or past life sessions, it often times can be simply learning to be happy, or work less, or to support a family member. Sometimes it's not so apparent what we are doing here, unless a person connects with their Master Guide, their Higher Self, or another spirit who knows your mission and destiny.

As I look back over life, I view my journey from a different perspective and with greater understanding – of course learning more as I go along each day: hindsight is 20/20. This world didn't randomly happen. I've come to know everything happens with a purpose—otherwise, *what is the point? Why do you exist? What's it all about?*

Looking forward helps keep a person in a fluid motion of their desires and destiny – keep your eye on your focus. If we believe the concept that there are no accidents and the universe is not a chaotic place but instead has divine purpose, we are able to view our lives from a different perspective. It may also help us to see ourselves in this Great Divine Plan.

One of the last of the Polynesian Kahuna's, Hale Makua, a very wise Hawaiian elder who we were introduced to by Hank Wesselman, left us these profound words, "We actually live in the past --- as the future came before. You must dream it first, then it happens."

When we lose our focus, then we can lose

our way—we can forget what we came to do –
we can lose touch with our mission. I can't stress
enough the importance for us to know what we
are doing here. Knowing our destiny and
following our path brings about a greater sense
of strength and peace within. I'm not at all
religious, but there is a beautiful biblical passage
which rings true, it states, "The peace that passes
understanding." In other words, there is a
calmness inside when we allow ourselves to
surpass our intellectual selves and know we are
guided.

The spiral does call you back in to re-look
at your life history. That's what the spiral is
about – your life story and your part of all of life's
story.

Tips to find your purpose:

1.) Explore the things you love to do and what flows within you when you are engaged in it.

2.) What qualities do you want to express the most in the world?

3.) Create a statement of your Life Purpose.

4.) What does your heart speak to you about? Identify it and then follow that inner guidance.

5.) Be clear about your life purpose – every thought, idea, or feeling that happens within you becomes a part of the fabric of the Earth's vibration and the Cosmic Universe. It's held within this fabric, so be very clear about what you put out there, as the Universe is listening closely

6.) Know what you're passionate about – what fills you up – then do it!

7.) What was it that left you feeling the most fulfillment?

8.) Define your goals, then align them with your purpose and your passions

9.) When you know what your passion and purpose is, don't let anyone or anything obstruct you from pursuing them. Remember, know where the opinion is coming from.

10.) Take action to set the wheels in motion

"A hundred years from now it will not matter what my bank account was...what car I drove...or where I lived, but rather the difference I made in another's life."

We can rarely know how we touch each other's lives; we may never know.

The following story takes place in 2010. My husband Bob and I were invited to Guanajuato, in Central Mexico. It was during the warm season there and my husband, who is an architect, was asked to redesign a place named the Lemuria Center. It was a small place and in the middle of nowhere, as far as I could tell. The owner Laurel had been in touch with a local high school at the time. She mentioned to us that the school was having difficulties with some of their students. There was a division amongst the students. Two rival gangs had emerged and had anger toward each other and were often fighting.

Laurel had been asked if she could help the students with this problem. Despite all efforts, they found no relief in the situation. The fighting had been going on all year and wasn't ceasing. Laurel explained the situation with us when we arrived in Mexico, and I asked, "what are they so angry about?"

She replied, "It's as if they have been fighting for centuries and don't even realize it's a different time. They're still holding a grudge from centuries long gone."

Laurel knew of our shamanic journey work and asked if we might guide a journey with the students. I thought, *This could be challenging, as I'm uncertain how to work with these teens, especially those I can't communicate with. Would they even be receptive?*

We were happy to help, but I must admit I wasn't sure it would make any sense to them. But I put my trust in spirit.

We entered the school and walked into the gymnasium. This was much the same as our high schools here in the States, although smaller. There were kids talking and moving through the halls, posters hanging from the walls, fairly the same as I remember when my children were growing up. I guess I had expected at most about twenty to thirty students and was quite surprised when we took a rough count of seventy-five students attending.

Laurel introduced us to the group, and we asked each student to get comfortable and to lie on the floor on top of the mats. They were still settling down and it took a bit to get them all quiet. You know how a large group of teens can be when gathered together. Now, I will say that I am not able to speak fluent Spanish, so Bob, who is fluent, interpreted at this point. As is my husband's way, he usually likes to connect with others by first having a little fun, which was perfect in this situation, and so his approach was no different with these teens. It was a good approach to break the ice and ease them into a new experience that they didn't understand.

I began explaining, in English, what this was all about, as my husband relayed it in Spanish, along with some humor. We could tell we were reaching the students and that they were relaxing. I explained what our intention for being there was, and about a shamanic journey. Because their culture is rich in ancient spiritual rituals, I realized it wasn't a far stretch for them to understand.

We asked each person to breathe in and out several times—as if you were intending to relax and fall asleep but remain awake. I then instructed each person to enter a quiet place within themselves and ask for the help of their ancestors and guides in order to heal the anger that many of them and their past generations felt. We began playing the instruments we brought—the native drum and an Australian Aboriginal didgeridoo. These sounds help to lower the brain wave frequencies in order to enter an altered state.

After a little time, we sensed that they were relaxed and on their way into this hypnotic state. I guided the journey while allowing the spirits to do the rest. When we finished and it was time to return, I played the drumbeat sound for the return. We watched as each student slowly awakened and began to move on their blanket.

I then asked if anyone wanted to share what they had seen in this journey. It was an amazing response. Many saw themselves as warriors laying down their bows and arrows. They didn't want to fight any longer. They felt a peaceful experience within this dream journey.

They saw resolution and how spirit could help with this problem. They asked, "how do you do this magic?" We explained it was their intention and focus that guided this journey with the help of the spirits and their ancestors, co-creating this to happen.

When we were finished and it was time to leave, they asked if we could return because it was so powerful for them and they wanted to learn more of this magic. We explained that we were visiting, but they could do it themselves. This felt like such a wonderful breakthrough and we thanked the spirits that facilitated this journey. I felt we could go with a feeling of peace.

Afterward, all three of us went for some lunch, because it's good to ground yourself when working in so much energy. A small man approached our table. He wore a t-shirt with a picture of Mother Mary on it. This isn't uncommon in Mexico. What was unusual is he spoke hardly any Spanish or English, only Mayan, but we muddled through a little conversation. Now, where we were in this region, there are no Mayan people living at this time, so we thought this was quite unusual.

We had a casual conversation and asked if he would like to join us for lunch. He replied, "No, but I'll take a bottle of water." He then asked, "What are you doing here?"

Bob explained in Spanish, about the school and the teens that were fighting for a long time with no resolve. The man replied, "You did good" and then left.

Within a moment, we all looked around and he had vanished. What's funny is there was no trace of him at all.

I thought, *Was he an angel? Had he been sent to acknowledge what we had done?* We'll never know for certain. But I did feel this was an acknowledging sign from the heavens that the spirits were pleased. This was truly a beautiful day.

The realization became clearer as the day went on—we are all a part of this very large community within the circle of life. It is our responsibility, as a part of the collective consciousness, to be and bring light and love. And so, it is!

Your connections to all the things around you helps to define who you are...

Food for thought

Have you found your purpose?
Are you a part of your community?

Chapter Six

Move the Bench

"In the questions of life, it is the quest that leads to the answer"

As an artist for many years, I've been trained to look at something from different angles, under different lighting, close up and farther away. Each one of these conditions creates a different perspective.

Let me say one thing here—perspective is

everything! It is about how we look at something. Do you wear rose-colored glasses or are yours clear? Do you always use your mind to determine your decisions or is there another option? Who can you trust to make the right decision? Where do the answers lie that you quest for? Think about this well-known question: Is the glass half empty or half full? Are you pessimistic or optimistic?

Years ago, there was a great commercial asking, "Is it real or is it Memorex? This was a type of recording tape, for those of you who aren't old enough to remember, which was advertised with the claim that a person couldn't tell the difference whether they were listening to a recording or the real deal. Have you ever put on a virtual reality headset and thought you were riding a roller coaster, when actually you were just sitting in your seat? It's about a point of view creating an impression—*perspective.*

Some people will ask their guru, their pastor, etcetera, for advice… there are many ways, to see things, none necessarily right or wrong. There is no magic solution. Why do we seek advice from others—going outside ourselves for our answers? Many times, the advice and our decisions are created from limited information, an opinion from others and driven by our habitual patterns or beliefs and fear, resulting with our becoming frustrated with life as we know it. We have the option—to seek a greater quality of existence by reaching and stretching into the unknown.

There are those, like me, who seek answers within, to receive guidance. I have several paths which lead me along my quest. One way is through shamanic journeying. It is guided usually by the sound of the drumbeat, rattle, soft flute, Tibetan singing bowls, or Aboriginal didgeridoo. These provide the vehicle upon which one can journey to non-ordinary realities.

Shamanism is the first known spiritual kind of practice of mankind and is known to actually date back thousands of years. A Shaman is a visionary who experiences the seen and unseen worlds, known also as the human and spirit worlds. In our culture we don't acknowledge the existence of these unseen realms, although more people today are opening to this concept, as was the case done centuries ago.

As the music provides the vehicle to get where we choose to go, it is through our intention which directs a person to have a specific journey. As known to shamans, the veil of our world and other realities is a thin barrier, whereby we can call upon spirits to provide guidance and help restore our power.

It is in this state of deep consciousness that our thinking takes a back seat in order for us to be able to use our senses. This is how we communicate with the spirits and guides, heal illness and help souls into the afterlife. Also, we can receive information or answers to questions—all of what we are searching for can be sought from within.

Dreams can be similar to a journey, but without conscious intention. Your dreams have your personal symbols and are unique to you. Information can be directed from your subconscious to your conscious mind through dreamtime, whereby messages can be conveyed. It is during sleep that each person has had this experience.

What comes to mind when I think of dreams are two classic movies that are familiar to all of us. Each is unique for the individual in the movie, and both have significant information to be conveyed, depending on the particular perspective.

The first movie is *It's A Wonderful Life*, where the main character George Bailey played by Jimmy Stewart, is unhappy and determined to change his life. He wants more out of his life than simply living in his dull hometown. He wants to go out and explore the world. When I watch or reflect on this movie, I see a man that is so determined to alter his life from what he has been dealt, but his destiny has other plans.

His angel named Clarence (his guide), comes to Earth to help him see his unsatisfactory life from a different perspective. The perspective being, *what if he hadn't ever been born?* All of the people whose lives he touched would be affected and altered. I believe this is why this movie is a long-time favorite, as like George Bailey, we all at times do not see the value of each of our lives. He was given an awesome opportunity to view his life from another perspective and then to use free will to choose.

Just like George Bailey, we all need extra help and guidance. We are not expected to do this dance on our own. *Where and how do you receive your guidance? How do you build a relationship with those that help you?* The way in which you might ask the advice of a friend or sibling.

The second movie that drives home a similar concept of perspective is *The Wizard of Oz.* This movie has been a favorite of many, as we all can identify with the characters and Dorothy's struggle in her search for the perfect place, somewhere over the rainbow. The characters all are a reflection of her in a symbolic way and offer guidance to assist her quest. She wishes to be loved and acknowledged more, to be a part of what's happening on the farm where she lives. As she sets out to run away from home and is faced with struggles and uncertainty, she insists on making her way back home.

During her quest, everyone tells her she must see the all-powerful wizard because he will know what to do. Along her way she meets those that can help her (guides) to get to see the wizard despite the many challenges they encounter — but they can't do the journey for her. When she finally arrives to see the all-knowing wizard—after a grueling task of retrieving the wicked witch's broom (symbolic of life's difficult challenges)—she realizes he's really not the wizard everyone thinks he is.

As I sit and ponder her journey, we realize Dorothy had the answers within her all along -as we all do-and as she was told in the end by a guide—the good witch — *"She simply had to learn it – accept it – and there it was."* In looking to someone else's opinion, she discovers that such an opinion is only as good as that source is. Dorothy realized the Wizard of Oz wasn't the powerful person everyone thought he was. *Does this remind you of a familiar situation?*

She had many helping guides along her path. Guides come in all shapes and sizes. She realized the wizard didn't hold the answers she needed, she needed to find them on her own, and finally figured things out for herself. At the end, she was able to articulate her desires and manifest her wishes.

Dorothy learned a lot in only one dream and so can we. Everything we see is a perspective, a viewpoint, but not always a truth, unless we *make* it our truth.

Laurie D. Wheeler

Now, having said all of this, I will share that I have been working in the unseen realm for over twenty-five years. I have learned much and have relationships with many spirits and guides whom I am so grateful to share my life.

The journey I'm about to share with you is one of the most profound experiences I've had in all of the years I've been journeying. The guidance shown to me, much like Dorothy, has been a foundational viewpoint and pivotal in my learning. The way I received the guidance is why it greatly impacted my life and the state I was in at the time, in which it anchored deeply within. I would like to share this journey with you.

It all begins with intention and the quest for information. This is one way I venture to find my answers within the unknown realms.

Years ago, I experienced a panic attack—as do many people—and had tried many different ways to avoid feeling like that again. However, once a fear etches itself within your memory it is quite difficult to change consciously.

On one particular afternoon, I was unusually anxious about what was happening in my life at the time. I decided to stop what I was doing at that moment to ask for help within. I started by playing my shamanic drum, which connects to the heartbeat and relaxing to me, and so this journey began, which I can recreate for you here.

After a few moments of conscious breathing and listening to the music, I journey into a deep, relaxed state. I am in complete control of where I want to go through my intention, guiding this journey, asking for guidance and know that I can return anytime. I begin some of my journeys by going to my safe and sacred place. I will describe this place so you can see why I might enjoy being there. Also, I will add that everything in this sacred place and reality is reflective of something about me. This is how we learn more about ourselves within.

I find myself in a garden with an abundance of plants, trees, bushes, grass, and a small water fall in front of me that empties into a small pool with fish in it. I can hear the sound of the water, and it's peaceful. As I look around, I see a small shed to the right, with a rooftop. I keep things in there I might want to retrieve to do garden work, the pruning of plant life *(internal changes)* while I'm visiting here. I notice there's a little monkey, the kind that the organ grinders have, it's staring at me. It's funny, when I observed it, it seemed very curious. This is one of my characteristics, I'm always wanting to know how and why, so the reflection of it is clear to me.

I have a fence that surrounds my garden from the outside world. I come often to this place as it is serene. I thought, *"If I want a guide to come and talk with me, I'll need a place for us to sit."*

In a moment, a park bench appears. It's made of wood with metal legs and its comfortable to sit on.

Now I'm ready to invite a spirit to sit with me so I can ask a question. This is how I might do it in my real world and so it is also for me in the invisible world. I have a clear intention at this time of what I want to ask and receive an answer to. I ask within my quiet mind, *"How do I change the fear I have that created my panic?"*

As I sit comfortably on my bench, within a few moments an image of a man appears. He is dressed in a floor-length black robe and wearing a five-corner hat. He has slanted eyes and long black hair with two small braids for a beard. He seems to be a kind and gentle spirit and represents a spirit with much wisdom. This is how spirits reveal themselves to us: it's our symbology that communicates the information.

He looks up at me and simply answers, *"Move the bench."*

Having worked with many spirits and guides, I know that Master spirits will many times speak with very few words. This is so you will ponder and absorb the information.

I thought, *this is it; this is the answer I receive to this important question? What am I supposed to do with this? What does this mean?*

It wasn't exactly what I wanted to hear.

As I reflected on these words, the information began to expand in my understanding. It occurred to me that I should look at this fear from another perspective. *But how do I do that? I've only looked at this from one way – the fearful way.*

I thanked him for listening and his words of wisdom, and then he disappeared.

I suppose, I need to sit and dive into this much more, I thought.

As the years have gone by, these words of wisdom continue to resound in my mind. By hearing this on such a deep level, this phrase has become the very foundation of how to view life when it's not clear, whether I'm working on a client case and at a stuck point; or am at a crossroads and unsure of which way to turn. Most importantly, I view fear in a different way. I continue to realize the fear I had was a matter of how I was perceiving it. When I looked deeper, I could see the blessings and richness of what it was bringing to my life and how I needed to adjust my thinking and feelings. The fear was a perspective that I was giving too much power to. Yes, there are times when it's appropriate to have certain thoughts and feelings, but I'm sure you'll agree, that we surrender our power to fear too often, I know I have.

We store some of these beliefs within us from our present time, and also brought in from another time, which may not serve us well. Our illusions or distorted beliefs may have served us well at the moment we had the original experience, as it became imprinted upon us, and now may be the time to view it differently. We must first, be willing to recognize and look at the fear or problem.

If you don't want to, it's ok, but the consequence is that it will remain unaltered. Choosing to face it is half the battle because then you diminish some of its power over you.

I've learned to ask myself; *how can I look at this differently and what is it I need to learn?* With help from inner guidance—and this is key—invite the information to come to me so that I can view it with honesty. Now, I may not always want or like what I hear. This, too, is a choice—but it's how I've learned to adjust my beliefs or any problems that need solving— by *moving the bench!*

Food for Thought

Are your glasses distorted or clear?

How do you discern your truth?

What beliefs or illusions do you have, that may no longer serve you?

Chapter Seven

Out on a Limb

Don't rush anything, when the time is right, it will happen! Timing is everything!

For some people, guidance is elusive. Others listen yet are fearful to trust. Then there are some who refuse to listen. And then there are times when we only get some pieces of the puzzle, making the answer unclear.

This is a wonderful story with a most

unusual ending. I've told it many times to many people and the reaction is usually similar—most will say, "that's so amazing." I happen to think so too! Timing is everything and is so synchronized...I couldn't possibly have thought this up.

Every year as I grow older, I look for some way during the Christmas season to give back to the community I live in. Years ago, in early October, I received an email from an unknown sender. Curiosity prompted me to open it. It was from a Native American tribe in the Dakotas on a particular reservation, asking for donations. The email explained that in the winter season, the people on their reservation often endured freezing temperatures—and some lived in actual tar paper shacks. As a sovereign nation, they are not recognized by our government and have an unemployment rate of ninety-six percent.

When I read this, I was appalled. As an American citizen, I didn't realize such a way of life could exist in the twenty-first century. I thought about these peoples' suffering and it touched my heart. I didn't know anyone who lived there, but all the same, I couldn't imagine that anyone should endure these conditions in this day and age.

For the last few years at this time, my husband and I would hold a gathering for people of the community and friends to come to our home where we would hold a shamanic journey together. It was a great learning for all of us and a wonderful time to grow as a community of like-minded people. I decided I would send an email to everyone that attended our group announcing, *I am collecting money and goods for the people on the reservation for the holiday.*

The response was overwhelmingly

awesome. People of the group shared the email with others, before I knew it, my home filled up—good news traveled fast. People brought coats, shoes, food, bedding, etcetera. It was so wonderful to see so many responding from a simple email. I felt blessed. Now you may be wondering, as I did, *how will I get all of these boxes to these people? This is an immense amount of goods, too heavy and too much to send by mail.*

Even though I felt compelled to make this commitment, I realized I had only thought so far into this endeavor and had not planned through all the necessary details (I hadn't thought there would be such a wonderful response). I couldn't think of a way to get thirty-six boxes of goods to the reservation without spending all the money I had collected to ship it. I thought, *I suppose it would be a shame to use all of this money for mailing.*

So, I called a special gathering of our journey group together one evening. It was a great meeting of many friends and a special time of sharing our ideas. This was to be a journey with one very specific intention for all of us —to discover a solution to get the donated goods to the intended destination.

We began by journeying into the unseen realm as I played the native drum. I could feel it was especially intense that evening, as the drum sang loud and strong. We all felt the vibe and it took us deep within. Everyone's energy was strong and vibrant. I felt confident that the spirits would guide us.

All of us who journeyed that evening either saw, heard or sensed some type of information. One person saw a white tractor trailer, and another saw a white bear. My guide, during the journey, reassured me to be patient, the answers would become revealed. Not always do the answers to questions come right away. It often becomes apparent in pieces as it unfolds for our learning experiences.

Despite having all of these puzzle pieces, we were still perplexed for a solution because none of us understood what all the symbology and images meant. We thanked our guides for the information and wrapped up our journey for the evening.

The next day, I was still sorting out the problem of how to get all of the goods to reservation. I didn't quite understand the information that came the night before, and was curious; *What was it telling me? What does a white truck and a white bear mean?*

I was trying to figure it all out with my mind, which is definitely not the way to do this. Usually, I was fairly good at discerning information and symbols, but this one confused me.

Two days later, I travelled up to Maine when I happened to wander into the back of a random store looking for a bottle of juice. There, as I looked to my right, I saw hanging on the community bulletin board, a flier printed on plain white paper showcasing a round circle with feathers hanging on the sides of it cut in four quarters. It was a symbol of the Native American Medicine Wheel and the four directions. On the bottom of the flier was some writing with a person's name, address and phone number.

I was amazed what was written on it. The person's name was Shirley Bear. It read that she helps certain tribes with food and clothing, along with all her information should you want to contact her for donations. Tingles washed over my whole body! I was ecstatic. I shed a few tears of joy and called her immediately, explaining the situation. I said, "I have all of these boxes filled with wonderful goods and I don't know how to get them out to this reservation."

She said she was filling a tractor trailer now, it was about three quarters full, to deliver goods out to this particular reservation in North Dakota in the next week. She advised that she had room to fit more for this scheduled delivery, and that she did this two times per year. I was astonished at how this all came together— desires and prayers were answered—and the rest is history.

The journey of a thousand steps begins with the first one!

All we needed to do was have a clear intention, ask for guidance, trust, and take action.

Know that there is power in numbers— when we come together with desire and intention, our goals will become powerfully amplified and are blessed. They, our guides, wait for us to call on them. And so, I am accustomed, after receiving to offer gratitude. I end my prayer with, *and so it is*. This is a respectful acknowledgement, as I know it is already in motion to happen.

This journey was clearly a teaching and learning for all of us, trusting each step of the way even when we don't know how it will all come together. Something within compelled me and I moved forward in action. During each step I was provided with the next clue and yet the whole puzzle was not revealed until it was time – yet another reminder that timing is everything!

Another point to this experience is that intention often determines what happens in life. At times I'm not always aware of how much this is so true. We may have great intentions and other times not so much, be careful of what you ask for. Life doesn't always show up in the way we want or expect, but remember that we co-create with All That Is, for the highest good. And therein lies the lesson.

I have had many experiences in life teaching me to trust. Over the years of my life, I've moved my home many times and needed to trust in order to take steps, often when it wasn't always comfortable, and I was unsure or fearful I was going the right way or making the right decision. I'm reminded of a movie with Harrison Ford as Indiana Jones. People are chasing him, and he comes to the edge of a cliff. He needs to trust, in order to take the next step to get away, and the steps have not quite manifested into reality. He must *step out on the limb.*

Life can be much like this pivotal moment. I have learned at times, the hardest lessons elicit the greatest gifts, all for my benefit. Maybe this is not always the way we think it should be or want it to be—leave out the expectations. Knowing this, I've learned to walk...*no*...leap into the unknown! Take the steps and be prepared for an adventure. This all can feel like a movie, unknowing how it will end going forward – but therein lies the magic! Life is about the journey, not the destination, and every day is an adventure.

When we were children, we all had times when we enjoyed pretending. As adults, it's wonderful when we get that opportunity to pretend by stepping out of the familiar to create who and what we want. There's a word I'm sure you may have used but as a child didn't truly understand beyond just saying it. The word is *abracadabra,* and it is from the Aramaic phrase meaning, "I will create what I speak."

Life is not always a matter of holding good cards, but sometimes, in playing a tough hand well...~ Robert Louis Stevenson

What simply stands in our way of hearing our guidance is a lack of trust. Many people I have spoken to over the years repeat the same questions and comments to me— I can't hear my guides." Or "I think they are there but I'm not sure. I'm afraid to trust. How do I know? I can't seem to connect with my guides."

And my reply is usually the same, "You've got to trust, if we don't trust we can't hear!"

I want to share a story about a young teen

named Steve. His parents had recently divorced and lived in separate towns. He wanted to remain in the same school system to continue with the familiar friends, teachers and education. Both parents wanted him to continue living with each of them and, as you can imagine, this was impossible. He needed to choose which parent he was to live with and finish his education. Steve happened to be enrolled in a VoTech year-long program. This particular program offered hands-on teaching in the automotive industry. He was an "A" student and had always had an eye for mechanics. Even at the young age of two and a half, he was always taking things apart and putting them back together – an inquisitive young one. His mother often wondered, *"How does a young child of this age have knowledge of putting something, intricate and complex, together?"*

He also had an imaginary friend who was always around him. His mother believed this was a guide, who was teaching him when he was young, possibly preparing him for when he got older.

At the time, his mom was moving to a home in a different school district, which meant everything in his life would change if he moved with her. On the other hand, if he lived with his father, he would remain in the school with his good friends and teachers that acknowledged his wonderful capabilities but wouldn't be living with his mom. This decision was particularly difficult for his mother, but she understood what was best for her son was to let him go and live with his father.

She and her son spent many times talking about it, but ultimately it was both their decision. She reached deep inside her heart and looked at the situation from the most important perspective—love. As a result, Steve went to live with his father and stayed in the school system to finish his education. This was only the beginning of what would unfold as a result of this important decision.

As the months rolled along, there was a national competition that was about to take place. Steve's teacher, Mr. G, had a keen sense of his students, with a true hands-on approach to teaching methods. Mr. G explained there was an automotive competition coming soon and only one team, comprised of only two students, could represent the school. Mr. G especially liked Steve, who was very interested and a responsible student. The first-place prize was five hundred dollars and an opportunity for the student to move forward and compete in the Worldwide Mechanics Competition. Teens from all over the country would gather to impress the judges with their knowledge and troubleshooting capabilities.

When the National competition took place, Steve and his partner won first place. They were so excited! This meant they could go on to the worldwide competition, representing themselves and their school. Although Steve's classmate was happy to win this competition, he felt it was too much for the next one. There was a two-month period of time that passed before this competition was to take place.

The day finally arrived when Steve was to be a part of this event. He was nervous and excited at the same time. Both his mother and teacher were confident that he would ace this, as he was good at problem solving.

As the competition was winding down, Steve was one of the last young men in the game.

The object was this: he was given a car that couldn't start. He was to find the exact problem and have the car running within a half hour. The tension mounted as time ticked by. It was only nine minutes in, when suddenly Steve got the car started.

The judges stopped the clock—they were amazed!

As they wondered, *"Did he cheat? How did he get this solved so quickly?"* The judges proceeded to examine the situation. It was unanimous! Steve won the competition! He took first place and was the worldwide champion. He was overwhelmed with excitement. He won a two-year scholarship to the college of his choice, an entire five-foot-high-toolbox, a new car, and cash. This was going to set him on a great path.

So, how did he arrive at solving the problem so quickly you might ask, as the judges did. I'm not even sure that he realizes the keen sense he uses for his problem solving, but I believe it comes from hearing within and trust, which he had learned at a young age. Therefore, he was guided along the path to his destiny. The money and prizes he won from the competition enabled him to further his education.

We'll never know what his path would have been had he not stayed in the school and won the competition. This was a part of his destiny. He furthered himself in this trade, graduated from college and eventually taught students at both high school and college levels, sharing and helping others along their path. Clearly, his mother also knew that he was meant to stay right where he was and continue what he was doing. This felt so right. She followed what she felt was the best for him, trusting even though it wasn't an easy decision.

When you face difficult times, know that challenges are not sent to destroy you, but instead they're sent to promote, increase and strengthen you. Focus on your strengths, find your talents, your passion, your destiny; and follow that path where it leads. Don't worry so much about what you can't do; just do what you can, as only *you* can do it.

As you develop your interests and they become your strengths, that strength becomes a purpose for you. Then you can let your imagination begin to roam...*where does it lead you to?* Play to your strength and allow your dreams to carry you through...

Food for Thought

Are you on the right path?

Is there anything or anyone obstructing your path? If so, how do you handle it?

Where and how do you receive your guidance?

Chapter Eight

Awaken Your Awesome

Just when the caterpillar thinks the world is over and goes into its cocoon....it becomes a butterfly!

The following is a heartwarming story about a young woman, or what I like to call a "cat with nine lives and she had used eight of them."

Kathy found her way to me in a peculiar way—isn't that how life can be at times? I often say, "As we're looking out the front door waiting for life to happen, the best things come in the back door."

Sometimes, a client will find their way to work with me in a way that I would never expect—and this is one of those times. This particular client, Kathy, had an addiction problem and had lost her way in life. Reeled in by drugs and alcohol, I believe she is a younger soul on a mission to find herself.

The Cat with Nine Lives

One day I was walking toward the beach when a woman about my age approached me from the opposite direction. We exchanged a pleasant hello and continued on our way. I remember having a bit of a twinge but didn't think anything of it at the moment.

About half an hour later, when I had turned around, I ran into her again. I could feel she was looking to start a conversation, and sure enough, she stopped and introduced herself, "Hi, my name is Dee. What a great day it is. Do you live around here?"

I said, "We're renting about three blocks away around the bend."

Dee said, "I didn't think you looked familiar."

I said, "I'm new to the area and just setting up my practice."

Dee asked, "What is it you do?"

I responded, "I'm a homeopath, which is holistic medicine."

She inquired more about it and, before I knew it, Dee began telling me about herself. She was a nurse, working in a hospital in Ohio and her husband was an orthopedic surgeon. They had two daughters, one of which was very troubled at the present time. I asked what that meant exactly.

As a homeopath, we are trained to always ask more questions and dig in deep, so it comes naturally.

Dee began telling me, "My daughter, Kathy, has been involved with a guy for a few years who is a drug dealer. She struggles with addiction to cocaine, she's an alcoholic, and at times she's depressed. She has attempted suicide on several occasions. She is angry and we have difficulty communicating. Kathy's been in several facilities but to no avail."

I thought, *"Wow, she's in a very difficult place."* And then something else came into my mind, *"This girl seems she's like a cat with nine lives and she's used up eight of them."* I felt Dee's desperation and the severity of the problem.

As Dee and I spoke further, I conveyed to her my compassion for her situation and said, "If there's anything I can do to help, please let me know."

This isn't uncommon for me to do because it's hard for me to hear of such a story and not want to help in some way. I gave her my business card and we went our separate ways. I really didn't think I would either hear or see her again.

Around 8:10 in the morning three weeks later, the phone rang – it was Dee.

She said, "I have a problem. Two nights ago, Kathy and I were having a fight and she pulled out a butcher knife from the kitchen drawer and came at me with it. I managed to run to my bedroom where my cellphone was on the chair and called the police and had her arrested. This wasn't the first time there were altercations at home." Dee explained, "I didn't know what to do at that moment, so they took her to jail. The judge now won't release her unless it's to a program. We've had her in three of the best facilities over the last couple years and nothing seems to work. Could you help her?"

I remembered what I felt when we had last talked a few weeks ago. I could hear the desperation in Dee's voice. And then I thought, *"What can I do? This is a tough one and I'm not sure if I'm capable of helping, this is severe."*

I wasn't sure I was prepared for this type of situation.

A voice came within me and spoke, *"You can help her, you are ready."*

I knew I wasn't thinking this up because just a moment before I was thinking the opposite. This sounded so difficult, but where would Dee get the kind of help that was needed.

I said I would need to think a bit on it, and

Laurie D. Wheeler

I would call back in a while. She agreed and I
hung up the phone.

This case was going to require an extra
amount of energy, trust, guidance and the right
conditions. I spoke with my husband and my two
children living home at the time because this
could affect them also. We all agreed it could
work and I phoned Dee back.

"Dee, this is Laurie. This will require
Kathy to sign a waiver, an exemption not to hold
me accountable for the outcome. I will do my
best, but I make no guarantees."

Dee and her husband agreed and a few
days later Kathy came to work with me.

Her parents had a cottage that wasn't too
far away from where I lived, so Kathy stayed
there. We worked together each day. I listened to
all of the information that she was willing to
share with me. I performed energy work with

her over the next weeks, coached her, gave her a homeopathic remedy for her addiction and taught her other tools that I thought would benefit her.

Within a month's time, there was a great shift. All of the hard work from both of us was paying off. I could see the change happening like a metamorphosis, a butterfly emerging out of the cocoon. There was life in her—her dreams and motivation were once again shining within her.

When it was finally time for Kathy to go home, her father came from Ohio to pick her up. When he arrived, we planned to go out for dinner. I could see he was so happy to reunite with her. At dinner, she told her father about what had happened over the last month and how she was excited to go home.

He remarked, "I've not seen Kathy look this good in many years."

Kathy felt confident enough to even have a small glass of wine to celebrate her remarkable change into a new person—or should I say *her true self.*

Now I know things can change and even reverse when people come out of a safe environment, but I felt confident in this situation and in Kathy. We spoke and had many follow-up sessions thereafter. She had remained in a good place.

Kathy talked about eventually opening up a clinic for others having these difficulties because she could now see how to help them. It was exciting to hear her wishes and feel she hadn't used all of her nine lives. Kathy went back to college and became a nurse, met a man, got married and had a baby girl. I lost track of her after time, although I'm convinced that she's in a better place today.

Kathy had an about face on her soul's path...I believe there are no accidents that happen in life. Everything has a purpose, even when we don't know or understand it. Listening and following is the key. What we do with it—knowing our purpose, keeping our focus—is all up to us. Kathy had chosen a difficult road but, with help, she changed her direction. I am very fortunate to have worked with her. I learned a lot about human nature and our will. It's incredibly inspiring to work this close and deeply with someone and watch the metamorphosis. I also have realized how deeply attached we are to our stories and how truly amazing the soul can change.

The following is a letter she wrote a while after she returned home and settled into her new life:

"I have been working

with Laurie for many months.
During this time, she has helped
me in many ways. Most
importantly, I have rediscovered
my inner self and have come to
a better understanding of my
life and those around me.

I have faced many
obstacles in my life. Although I
have a wonderful family, my
genetic gene pool is not the
best. There is a history of
mental illnesses, such as severe
depression and paranoid
schizophrenia, obsessive
compulsive disorder, alcoholism
and eating disorders on my
paternal side. On my maternal
side, there is also a history of

depression since I was seventeen and am now twenty-four, I have been obsessive and compulsive as long as I can remember and most recently, I had been using drugs and drinking large amounts of alcohol regularly. I was also in an unhealthy relationship and have been sinking lower and lower this past year.

On Easter morning of 2002 I was at home visiting my family. After a long week of using large amounts of cocaine and consuming unreasonable amounts of alcohol. I was ready to relax in the comfort of my parent's home. However, things did not work out that way. From my understanding, my parents could not wake me up that morning and became concerned, so they kept on checking on me. My father, an orthopedic surgeon, noticed that I was turning blue and when he came close, realized I was barely breathing. I woke in the ICU of the hospital. I was told I almost died. My self-destructive lifestyle was catching up to me. Due to the alcohol and drugs in my system, a doctor at the hospital suggested rehab.

So, I went to one of the best in the country. There my

depression grew even more
severe. I felt that I didn't really
relate to others there and felt so
alone. Desperate, I attempted to
slit my wrists, thinking death
was my only option. Thankfully,
I survived, but I was still
unhappy. A few months later
Laurie came into my life.

The first time I met her, I
felt very comfortable. However,
I had a hard time trusting
people and it wasn't easy for me
to open up. I also wasn't sure
what to expect and maybe she
was like all the other
"therapists" I had seen. Instead
of just writing a prescription
such as Prozac or Effexor (I've

been on at lease 10 different antidepressants) or telling me to go to AA meetings, I felt Laurie actually cared and truly listened to me. She is the first person that I have ever opened up to completely.

Laurie and I discussed events from my childhood to my present life. She listened to me and asked questions that really make me think, allowing me to express what I was feeling and why at certain times in my life. Laurie also asked me to write down my dreams. It is amazing the significance that they have. She is able to explain the meanings behind them.

After getting to know me better and learning about me, Laurie researched what remedies she thought would help me. She put a lot of time in deciding what remedy I would benefit most from. I am very happy with the results. The remedy I took helped me to begin healing from within. I discussed daily with her the changes I was feeling. Each day I felt better and more confident. Not only is my mental state improved, but I feel and look physically better.

I feel honored to have worked with her. She has a special gift in helping people.

Laurie D. Wheeler

Laurie reminded me that life is
an adventure and a learning
experience. I choose what paths
I will follow on my journey
through life. With her help, I
have learned to moderate things
in my life and not be so extreme.
I can honestly say that I am
happy and look forward to my
future. I am confident that I can
face any obstacles that I come
across. I don't think that I could
have come to this inner peace
without Laurie's help. I am
truly thankful for the time we
spent together. I write this for
others so they can know that
change is possible." – Kathy
12/12/02

You're not stuck. You're just committed to certain patterns of behavior because they helped you in the past. Now those behaviors have become more harmful than helpful. The reason why you can't move forward is because you keep applying an old formula to a new level in your life. Change the formula to get a different result.
- Emily Maroutian

The Butterfly Emerges

The following is a story that is near and dear to my heart. I write this because this, too, is about a young soul, the choices that were made, and realigning with her purpose in life by awakening to who she really is.

It was July 1, a few days before the holiday

when I was sitting in meditation. I had a vision that was very upsetting. I saw a small white car with a couple of young people in it, but I couldn't make out the faces. They were driving down a highway and were hit by another car. I suddenly came out of the meditation because it was so startling. At that time in my life, I didn't realize I could re-enter a dream to either see more or to alter dreams. It bothered for the next day but then I forgot about it.

I was at work on the hot morning of July 3 when I received a phone call from my son, "Sara's been in a car accident in New Jersey." The hospital had called the house and he had picked up the phone. "She's in the emergency room but they don't know how bad it is yet."

This came as quite a blow. No one ever likes these kind of phone calls. I quickly went home to get my son and we drove to the hospital, which was two hours away.

At this point, I need to back up into the story to explain more. Sara was sixteen and having some rough times in life, as many teens at this age do. She had some troubling experiences prior to this particular age, which had impacted her self-esteem and confidence. At this fragile stage in her development there were people influencing her decisions, which I feel led up to this event. She wasn't hanging with kids that were making good choices. Sara was involved with drinking a lot which added to depression and missing a lot of school time. This was going on for about two years and had culminated to this point in her life.

As her mother, I was deeply concerned about her welfare because she was living with her father at this time and was often times unsupervised. So, as you can see, the build-up to this moment in time was a train wreck waiting to happen. You can imagine all the fears and visions going through my head as I made my way to the hospital.

Eventually, I arrived and made my way into the emergency room. I spoke with the attending nurse and it seemed that they were still trying to get more information. The nurse walked me into the room where my daughter was lying there banged and bruised and exhausted.

She was very groggy, and I asked, "What happened?"

She responded in a low and slow voice, "I was in the passenger seat with her friend Kylie who was driving. They were singing to the radio and this guy pulls into their lane hitting the car on her side, the car spun and then crashed. Kylie was fine, but I blacked out till the ambulance arrived."

I was so happy to see her, but she was pretty banged up. I wanted to know more and what lurked under the surface was still a mystery.

It was then that I strongly felt the need to find out what had really happened. As Sara didn't have any recollection from the black out, I needed to know what was going on. It seemed things had really spiraled out of control. I asked her if it was ok and I laid my hands on her to hear from the spirits. This is what I heard and saw.

A very large and radiant angel came to my vision. Its glow was illuminating, and it had wings! I didn't even bother to ask its name as it was so majestic, and I was in awe. It said to me that Sara was going to be fine. She had been in a place between time where she met with her guides. This is a realm where time seems to stand still as it felt at this moment. There the question was posed to her, "Do you want to stay or leave this lifetime?"

Her angel said that she agreed to stay and do the work and live her purpose for which she came for. It also said, "You are her mother, your task is to support her as she will need, in order for her to achieve her purpose."

At that moment, I remembered back before she was born. I remembered how I knew her before I met her and how much I wanted to be together again. My heart ached to feel this. It was too soon for her to leave and I was completely overwhelmed and overjoyed that she made that decision. This was a day to write about in the baby book. It was a turning point for her. It took some time to push through, but she took the steps.

Today, Sara is a mental health counselor, a mother of two beautiful children and helping guide others along their path.

I learned that day about the soul, about love, about the choices we make and how fragile and difficult life is. I knew Sara. I knew what a sweet and beautiful person she truly is and that she has wonderful and important things to still do in the world. As I've always told her, "You're a force to be reckoned with," and now she lives up to that in her life.

Life's twists and turns take us down a path and sometimes we all go astray. I was so grateful for the angel to come and share the warmth, the love and information. It helped me to understand how to continue along as her mother and that Sara had planned her life this way in order to evolve. When life is difficult and it presents with obstacles and you can't find your way, here are some helpful tips:

One, know that you planned it for a good purpose. This is no random accident.

Two, the more difficult lives are the ones we do the most growing through.

Three, when you're not on your path, it's your choice to wake or not. There's no one telling you what you must do. If you decide not to stay here and finish what you came for, you will return to do it again.

Four, some type of help is always there, all you need do is ask and trust.

I'll share my favorite quote with you because it has been a great inspiration over the years to me. I believe this is what it is to be a butterfly emerging from its cocoon. I know it's what a soul feels when it finds its true self and purpose.

"When you are inspired by some great purpose, some extraordinary project, all your thoughts break their bonds; your mind transcends limitations, your consciousness expands in every direction, and you find yourself in a new, great and wonderful world. Dormant forces, faculties and talents become alive and you discover yourself to be a greater person by far than you ever dreamed yourself to be." ~ Pantanjali

Food for Thought

All of life is a learning experience, are you ready to learn who you really are?

Do you know what lessons you've come to learn?

Chapter Nine

What's It All About?

"To be or not to be"

The path isn't a straight line—it's a spiral... continuously coming back to things you thought you understood so you can see deeper truths.

I would like to share more background about souls before telling this next story. All souls do not originate from this planet. There are those that primarily originate from either another planet, another galaxy or universe – the celestial realm. Those who continue to incarnate here, time after time, we'll call Earth-Based souls or EBs. Some souls who originate from these other realms we'll call InterPlanetary souls or IPs.

An InterPlanetary soul is a soul who has not inhabited here on Earth more than a few times and is from another celestial place. I know this because I have worked with some, although they do not have conscious knowledge of being this type of person, the information becomes apparent during our work together. I am an IP soul and have learned this personally, through my own past life regressions, energy work, channeling or journey work. As the awareness of my own soul has grown, I have actually become more sensitive to other IPs, sometimes sensing before they know themselves, which helps me to address either sharing information or working together from a different approach— *move the bench.*

When an IP has embodied on Earth, there are distinct challenges to overcome. This is due to an IP's unique and evolved lifestyle, presenting IPs with behaviors and customs here on Earth that are foreign to our original home base. Many times, IPs come to Earth alone, without members of our soul family. Although, at times IPs will incarnate with another member of the same soul pod, as a child or parent to help assist each of us in our mission. An IP will often be a scout for our own soul's home, preparing and learning about obstacles, that we may further encounter on Earth.

Unique for IPs, we often have a different form of communication, unlike Earth, sometimes without any human sensory channels or physical interaction, and is therefore a method which bypasses the ego filters.

IPs are benevolent in nature and bring what we know from our soul's home to Earth, as usually we are from a world which approaches life in a different manner. IPs are often from other worlds and realities which many times are without anger, sadness, wars, fighting, judgement, etcetera...and are therefore more in sync with the true nature of the soul. Quite simply, IPs find difficulty in understanding why people of Earth do what they do. What we learn on Earth is also reciprocal in nature, there are important lessons for us to learn while we are here doing our work.

I have received this information and been advised, as a part of the Divine Plan, by connecting to spirits and extraterrestrials, that we must do our work in order to move through the third dimension. On Earth, we live in the third dimension currently, which will no longer serve the way of life on Earth in the future. Third dimension is filled with judgement, anger, and deep wounds of separation. As a part of this great universal plan, we will move beyond the fourth dimension which is similar to the third, still very much connected to the 'ego'. The fifth dimension opens us to a higher vibration, liberating Earth and living amongst celestial spirits, filling us with compassion, kindness, and consideration.

In keeping with this, there are those of a higher vibration or lower density that are simultaneously adjusting their personal and their world vibration. I believe this is the reason we all on Earth presently experience such intense feelings because we must transmute these vibrational frequencies (thoughts and emotions) that will no longer serve us in order to evolve. When we transmute something, we achieve a change in its form, nature or substance. In our current time on Earth, there are more IPs here to help the people and the planet, than have been at other times, as this now is greatly needed.

There are also souls who have had many lives on Earth, and they are known as Earth-Based souls or EBs. They have incarnated many times and remain here time after time to progress humanity. In the universes, we are all learning, no matter where we are from, and it's all happening simultaneously, received and sharing through the collective consciousness. It's a vast existence and we're all a part of it.

Moving on, I would like to talk a bit about past life and between lives soul regression. Using hypnosis, which achieves a state similar to meditation, this process supports and guides a person into a relaxed and altered state of consciousness. This is achieved by guiding them into a lower brain wave frequency, which we do daily on waking and falling asleep. An awake and conscious state is the Beta state. Then, as we are relaxing further, we fall into an Alpha and then Theta state.

It is here in these deeper states of consciousness that a person's other lives and aspects of self can be revealed. During this time, a person may connect with guides and what is known as the "Library of Wisdom or the Akashic Records". This is known to be a collection of all human events, thoughts, words, and emotions, and a source which unveils true information. It is in this reality where a person can connect to the unseen realms, learn of their soul's wisdom, and meet their Higher Self, receive guidance from spirits, and learn of the soul's origin.

Understanding the Self

The following tells of a past life and between lives soul regression I guided for Stephanie, who clearly is not originally from our Earth, but an IP soul, although initially she possessed no clue of this consciously. I knew the moment I met her she was an InterPlanetary soul.

This regression illustrates how an IP can learn by embodying on Earth, and the challenges she or he faces in doing so.

Stephanie, a woman around forty-five years old, stepped into my office and was a bit uncomfortable about doing a regression. She expressed to me that she was interested in doing a regression but wasn't sure she would be induced into a hypnotic state and uncertain about what she would gain from the process. I reassured her I felt confident I would be able to help her access some answers and mentioned she was in control of the process and could stop at any time.

I stated, "All hypnosis is self-hypnosis and all of the guides and I have your best interests at heart."

She relaxed a little and we proceeded with the interview.

She sat in the comfortable chair and began to relax, but I could still detect some discomfort. Upon inquiring further, I asked if there was another reason why she was still uncomfortable? She replied, "I'm not sure if I want to know what I'm about to experience, but there is another part of me that does want to know."

She began to tell me more about herself and the illness she had - Lyme disease, for fifteen years. She explained she didn't understand why or how to heal from it, and that nothing was working.

Having been with many clients over twenty-five years, I was quite familiar with her situation and understood how difficult it must be for her. I explained to her that I felt a regression would greatly benefit her. This type of session would allow her to ask direct questions and experience what her lessons were about.

As I talked her down into a relaxed hypnotic state that helped her to relax and sink into the comfortable chair, she described that she found herself in a luminous white hallway where there was a brilliant white rounded door and everything blending together—it was simply all light.

Stephanie said, "This is coming to me telepathically. They don't want me to spend too much energy or time on this or material things because I can become too attached."

I asked her to open the door in front of her. She stated she only had to think it and it slides opens like the doors do on Star Trek. She said, "I only have to ask for something and it will appear."

Stephanie proceeded to open the door. It opened into a lush jungle with plants surrounding her. She said, "There are what feels to be a lot of presence of spirits and life here. There are animals and the plants are talking to me and I'm aware of their awareness of me."

She was greeted by birds, animals and

vegetation and she became busy connecting with everything. She said, "I can smell the mistiness of the air, I feel the breeze on me, and I am barefoot with a long, flowing simple white cotton dress."

She said, "I am a female, not of a particular age, wearing a gold chain with a crystal diamond around my neck. My hair is long, and my face cannot be seen as it is very light, like a pale translucent. It changes with what my intention is. I cannot really feel my body because I am a spirit being, emanating light and vibration. It is why nature can speak with me, as we are all One." She continued, "It feels very small, tight and dense in here *(she refers to her physical body)*, it makes me feel nauseous. I don't feel well, I want to burst out of it and be who I am. I want to be my essence. My body is suffering too much. I have not been here many times, and this is why it's so challenging."

Stephanie continued to share what she was hearing while in her regressed state, "It is easy to fall into these stories here on Earth. I don't want to live out life in a story with humans. I am working to rid myself of attachments and my story. My essence has been in service long enough. I realize my limitations, and this is not natural for me here, though I would like to help more people, I feel I want to leave now. It is hard to let go of people; they make it hard to say good-bye. My guides further tell me, we are heading into challenging times, which will be very hard. It will get worse before it gets better. I know this already and it makes me sad. I don't understand this reality—it's too dense and I'm tired of being here. Although people have good hearts, it feels like a different consciousness than where I am from. I don't want to play this story anymore."

Her guides further told her that she

needed to understand what it is like to be 'stuck.' She said, "I am here to help people to move into lighter ways. People think they need to be attached, but there's much more to it than that and we need to remember where we are from. I remember I'm from a very far galaxy."

She continued to describe her galaxy, "It has a blue and violet indigo tone with a lilac mix. It feels so good, like being One and there is a lot of peace there. I remember being on other planet forms where there are water forms and I like that. I am detaching so much while I'm here on Earth that I didn't realize how attached I was."

Stephanie told me that there are many different planets and celestial places working with Earth, bringing help and neutralizing tensions. They want to come here but the situation is confusing to all that are not from Earth. There are many that bring benevolence.

There are those that are making decisions now for Earth. Stephanie states that if she gets too attached to her Earth story it will be difficult for her to return home.

She continued, "My illness helps me to bring light to the planet, as there is much disease. I had to let the illness come deep inside of me, to attach to it, to be human and create this frequency on a cellular level. There are so many that have this disease. We can't let the darker entities from other frequencies know. This is why we need the white light frequencies. To let go is harder than simple thought because we believe so much in our attachments, we believe the stories. Without that attachment, my own essence can push back and destroy this illness."

As Stephanie traveled from the above experience, she then spontaneously moved into a reincarnation.

"Now I feel myself incarnating to a time period. It is World War II. They have difficult torture methods. This humanity is confusing for me. They are conducting medical experiments. I feel that my soul enters into different bodies. I'm hiding now and I can see black boots. They take me to the gas chambers, and I can feel the collective fear, there is so much darkness of the people, the villagers. This is challenging and I feel their despair.

I feel a tarry vibration in my body, and it is much like the way my illness feels today. I am very attached to this experience. We must stop the torture of human species. There are benevolent species here working to help everyone, so I need to accept the detachment. I will miss these people, but I must detach in order to bring light and feel more of the collective consciousness."

Stephanie now entered the death scene as she has finished with that life period. Her soul floated away from her dead body. She said the color of her soul is a collective indigo blue purple. She can easily connect with other forms of vibration, and some of these forms are white light. Now, as she described, she integrates into a more benevolent collective consciousness and there is less pain now when she is in this state.

She stated that it was very soothing, especially on her right side, where her pain is usually more intense. She described finding herself in an expansive state. Her pain was transmuted more easily now in this state because she had gained access to the violet purple indigo light which also helps to heal her (this is her Higher Self). This was happening more as she integrated with the color and vibration. She could feel it in her cells and her spinal fluid. She is able to easily transcend the pain and change it, from this state.

She now told me that she had neutralized multiple lifetimes through this experience and was completing Karmic debt—because she's now able to let go. The more she let go of the emotional experience, the more she was able to become a vessel to transmute the co-infection and its progression in this Earth dimension.

She said, "For the next generations it will be harder, as they are so attached on so many levels. I am here to bring energy in, break the negative energy down and transmute it. This is my purpose for this lifetime on Earth."

After Stephanie finished her regression session, she realized and understood so much more. She now knows herself to be an InterPlanetary soul, and what her mission is, and release her story.

As she has worked at transmuting the energy of her illness, it is important for us, also, to let go of our stories, our illusions and not remain attached, as it can ultimately become too painful both mentally and physically for us. No matter whether an IP or any other soul, when we don't release our stories, we carry them and their pain within our soul and subsequently incarnate with this energy. Like Stephanie, we must transmute and heal.

This regression helped Stephanie to understand why she was in so much pain. She received a deeper understanding of herself as an IP. Her soul's origin became apparent immediately as she stepped through the door into another reality. The essence of her soul was light, benevolent and free but heavy and sick while she is here on Earth due to her story. Part of her mission was to know she must let go. She found answers to her burning questions and even more, with this guidance, she was able to access them. When she emerged from the hypnotic state, Stephanie stated that more than fifty percent of her pain had diminished, and she felt so much better.

This particular session reinforced how we are all attached to our stories. Our illusions are much like being in a movie that we create and are for us to learn from and then we must let them go.

That's what the spiral is, your life story, all of life's story... **this is what it's all about.**

"You cannot suffer the past or future because they do not exist in the present moment. What your suffering is your memory and your imagination - Sadhaguru

Laurie D. Wheeler

Food for Thought

Have you ever wondered who you are without the stories you tell yourself?

What are you doing to let go of your stories?

Do you suffer with an illness that might be a part of your story?

Chapter Ten

Do you know who you really are?

"You are never too old to set another goal or to dream a new dream"

- C. S. Lewis

The following story is of an older woman whom I met at a convention. As she shared with me her anxiety and sorrow about thinking that she is an alien abductee and believing that much of her life has been wiped away, I couldn't help but feel I might be able to help unlock some mysteries and try to connect the dots.

Carol flew in from Texas on a Thursday morning and came directly to my office in Santa Fe, New Mexico. She felt hopeful that I might be able to regress her in order to help her find answers to her questions. I mentioned that it might also be helpful to uncover and move the energy in a session before we do a regression. She agreed, so that Thursday morning we started with some energy work.

As she sat in the soft chair in front of my desk, Carol told me what questions she wanted answered. She said, "I believe I'm an alien abductee and I want to know what is the ET's intention? Why have they blocked my memory, as it has been wiped away? I feel drained of some of my happiness, and how do I get it back? If they have done so, how do they take my DNA? Why do they still want me at my present age? What is my connection to this cosmic lineage and ancestry, and has there been extraterrestrial DNA manipulation with my own children and grandchildren? I hear such manipulations run in families for generations."

After the interview and hearing her concerns, I asked her to get on the massage table so that I could begin the energy session. She did so, and I covered Carol with a blanket and placed some drops of flower essences in the palm of her hand. These essences help her to connect with the spirit world, to enhance awareness of her Higher Self, and to be open to spiritual gifts, as well as to impart knowledge, and achieve trust. I then asked her to hold two quartz crystals in her hands and began to play a musical recording. The music of the native drumbeat began to play, allowing Carol to be guided into a hypnotic trance state. Often in these sessions, we do not speak until after the session. So, I don't know what she experiences, and she doesn't receive any input from me until we share such information at the end of the session, and so I was prepared with pen and pad next to me, to record information.

As I began my energy work, I called upon my guides and asked for power, protection and support. Then I placed my hands on her feet to begin facilitating the energy. In a moment, I began to see in my vision that emerged, a table with Carol laying on it. There were three surgeons wearing surgical masks and standing around the table. They have performed a surgery and were sewing her abdomen area. The energy was extremely strong in this area of her body and some of the surgeons were therefore moving away from her. I then saw an ET, gray, standing about four feet tall, with large black eyes and a slit for a mouth. It said to me as it stood right in my face, "Do not interfere with our work."

I exclaimed, "Do not hurt her, she is a soul and you don't have the right to hurt her. Her soul deserves to be free."

At that moment, I was taken aback by what I had actually said, and thought to myself, *"I am being quite bold in saying this as I'm not quite sure of their intentions. How do I know if they are friendly or not? I hadn't even hesitated to answer back in this way."*

I then saw the alien and he was creating some sort of musical tones. I continued to say, "Her soul is free to choose, and I would like to facilitate her healing now."

A few moments passed by and again the ET said, "Do not interfere with our work here."

I then saw Carol with a blanket wrapped all around her, wrestling to try to get out of it.

She then exclaimed, "No, I don't want you to."

I felt she was referring to either being impregnated or some type of harvesting of her female eggs. Regardless, she didn't want them to do what they were intending to do.

Carol had advised me during her interview that she has five children that she has physically birthed, four of which she claimed are ET hybrid children. At this point, I could see that they had taken a third baby from her, and that it was neither a male nor female, but I could not otherwise really make out what it looked like. I also heard in my vision that they had disrupted or altered her female organs in order to do their work.

The ET Gray returned again and stood in front of me.

I started to say, "Leave her..." and then I heard a voice. The voice said to me, "Don't get angry, you will lose your power, instead ask the light to come."

I realize the truth of this information immediately and let go of the anger I was feeling. If I was to keep my power and facilitate the job I was to do, then getting upset wouldn't allow for that. Yet, this felt like such an injustice, as I was there on behalf of her soul. I then asked for the light to enter and continued facilitating the energy, knowing the light would be what was needed.

In the next moment, I saw the front of a Catholic church with a very important leader. He was wearing a black robe and a mitre. A mitre is the official headdress worn in ceremonies by bishops and abbots in traditional Christianity. I saw Carol at about seven years old, kneeling down at the altar receiving communion. I noticed something dark in the bottom left corner of my view of the scene. It was all gray black, wearing no clothing, it looked like something out of a sci-fi movie, and it didn't have a good vibe. I then had the feeling that this dark entity wanted something Carol had. It said it wanted her innocence and her soul.

Then I was in the next scene, which happened as I am working around her throat and head area, doing my energy work. I heard there were codes that were being uploaded to her. I asked, "How do they upload to her?"

I received the explanation that her DNA is encoded and therefore carried on throughout her lineage. I then felt the movement of energy wrapping and encapsulating her body. All information had halted, and it was clear we were finished. The energy and information we both received was now complete.

At this point, Carol was ready to get up

from the table. I asked her what she had experienced. She began telling me, "I saw snowflakes, but they were more like stars, bright white light, and there were about forty to fifty of them, coming and going. They had a bit of gold light to them and it was so beautiful. I then saw a purple light and it filled all of my field of my vision, and it was soothing."

She continued, "I then see symbols, like what you might see on a teepee. But they weren't American Indian. She began to draw these on my note pad. One was a round circle with a line, then a larger line in it and a small circle also inside. The next was like an arrow with something like the letter 't' at the end of it. She continued, "I don't know what these symbols mean or why I saw them. I then saw something round like a sun and noted that some of these figures appeared as if they could have faces in them, but I didn't see a face.

Carol then said, "When you were working around my belly, I felt some cramping, which I hadn't felt since I was a younger woman. I saw a face with a pair of slit-like dark, black eyes, and a line where a mouth should be. I don't remember anything else."

We both sat and talked for a while longer about her experience. She then shared more information about her children and her life's experiences. Her suspicions were that she's been abducted by aliens for most of her entire life. In fact, she shared that not only she, but her children, her mother, aunt, father and grandfather have all been abductees. Her first son, born Autistic, as a young child would see stars and talk about space. She also feels her sisters' twin children actually are her own children but were born of her sister.

I expressed a few thoughts about her children and how it might connect to the energy session, noting that the information in the received form of such symbology is not always clear or easy to interpret. The energy and spirits will facilitate what needs to happen, but the information can reveal itself over a period of time thereafter. I was certain more information would come through the Past Life and Between Lives Soul Regression the next day. Carol left feeling refreshed and happy for the experience and the information which was conveyed. She hoped she might hear something during her dreams, though she rarely dreams, or rarely has any visions.

The next day, Carol came into my office happy. She said, "I'm really looking forward to this regression. I didn't have any visions last night, but I slept very well and feel great today."

I had asked Carol, prior to the session, to make a list of five questions she would like answers.

She said, "I have so many I don't know where to begin."

I replied, "Tell me what you'd like to know, and I will ask accordingly. Sometimes answers will be revealed within the events that take place during the regression."

I asked her to relax and began to guide her into a relaxed state, always reminding her that she was in a safe place and in control of this hypnosis. In a few moments Carol reported that she found herself in a dark room with a bit of light coming in, but there were no windows.

She said, "It is me who is lighting up this room. I'm like a ball of light and I have complete peace. I'm looking for someone to help me, I feel lost, not knowing my true identity. I know I am valuable and loved but I can't find anyone in this room that agrees. In the corner there is a small spirit and I recognize him. I saw his face in an art museum and I instantly recognized him. He doesn't feel good to me. He wants something. He says he wants my soul, but I won't give it away. He's staring at me, as I haven't seen him in a while, since June at the museum. He sees something he really wants for himself. He looks like an ogre, not pleasant looking. He's gray and black and very small about two feet tall. It seems he's of a lower level of creation than me. He wants my love and laughter. I tell him to go away and he does. I didn't know I could say that. I see the door again and a man walks through. I feel goodness and light, and I don't fear him. He is dressed like a priest; a very holy man come to help me."

He asked, "Would you like to go to the

garden with me?"

I said, "Yes."

Now we are in a garden, with flowers and greenery and there is a cement bench to sit on. We sit and admire the beauty.

I asked, "Who are you?"

He answered, "I am you. You are greatly loved and valued, do not question that."

I am taking in what he says, and I ask, "What are your accomplishments, why are you here with me?"

He said, "To convey light and love and gentleness and good will and peace to your spirit"."

Carol said, "I am now feeling like I understand, I feel grace, I feel accepted and loved."

I ask Carol to ask this spirit (her Higher Self) how she is to recognize this spirit is with her.

The spirit responded, "By being your true self".

I ask on Carol's behalf, "How does she access this?"

It responds again, "Remember the nine fruits of the spirit. Then Carol adds that, "The spirit promises to leave little tokens, here and there, for me to find, they are from him, to remind me of its love for me."

Then Carol gently thanks him, and weeps.

I gently begin to weave together this information with the questions that Carol had come to my office with while continuing to address questions to her spirit. I asked, "What intentions do the extraterrestrials have"?

It said, "The gifts have been given that others want – empathy – faith – goodness – gentleness they come from you heart chakra".

I asked, "What drains her happiness?"

It said, "Sometimes Carol allows her lower self to let this happen. She feels sorry for herself and is drawn away from the light."

Carol then expressed, "That ogre, he's responsible in some way but I banished him..."

The guide then stated, "Say the word Bethlehem, which means the city of bread and the Bread of Life is the light."

I inquired further, "Why have the ETs blocked Carol's memory?"

The spirit then spoke through Carol, who said as she smiled feeling the love of her spirit, "Nearly all of her memory has been wiped away."

I asked, "Why?"

It said, "They do not have emotion like humankind, they take the memory or almost all, without conscience. They want it to make their world and all worlds higher and brighter. They take what we have for their own and add it into their consciousness." Carol added, "It's for my benefit".

I asked, "How is it for Carols benefit?"

It replied, "To be spared what might be grotesque and terrifying."

I further asked, "Why do you still want to abduct her?"

There was silence.

Carol replied as the spirit spoke through her once again, "It is unknown, no answer."

I then asked, "How do they take her DNA?"

It replied, "They take her eggs".

As I moved from some of the questions Carol wrote on her paper, I wanted to inquire about the codes that were revealed yesterday during the energy work. I asked, "Can you tell about the codes from yesterday?"

It replied, "They are ancient, they move through the ethers of Carol's imaginations. She can see instantly and recognize they are tiny but there. One of them is a universal music symbol. Some of them are codes of her DNA of all of her incarnations."

Carol then begins to speak for herself and said, "I can see what they look like, it's like an alphabet and some can be organized into a language and they move freely out and into my imagination. Now they are gone."

Carol now stated, "I can see pyramids and a beautiful river, homes, gardens and a whole society. I am on another planet."

I asked, "Where are you, what is the name of the place you are in?"

Carol replied, "Anexa. I see two groups of people. One is more human-like and the other are from somewhere else but came here to help other people. I live here and have a happy life. I am of the first group of people." Carol said this knowledge filled her with ecstasy.

When the regression is finished, I asked Carol a few more questions in order for this experience to become deeply anchored within herself. I asked her, "What have you gained most from this experience?"

She replied, "I have gained the wisdom of the priest, as my Higher Self. I understand for a long time, across many lifetimes, I have been a seeker of truth, light, all things good. This was confirmed today, and I am to continue to bring goodness to others and to the planet."

I further asked her, "What possibilities do you see that are open to you now?"

Carol replied, "I need to speak up when I sense the extraterrestrials come. I never could say anything until yesterday's energy session, and I am convinced of this need, even more today. I must draw clear boundaries and disinvite them from taking, taking, and taking from me. They may have purpose, but they need to realize they are having a harmful effect on the human soul. They need to find the door and leave me. I am also clearer on relationships that no longer serve me well. I can be influenced by those beings who keep their thumb on me, who control me. I am free from that now."

I felt that at this moment the truth had been revealed for her – she got it! She felt more empowered and was able to connect the dots.

Carol further replied, "The whole experience is one of purification, from the illusions, and rising above them to who we really are."

I was so inspired and elated by her experience.

Carol went on to say when she does dream, which isn't often at all, she's in the ethers and checking on the energy grid, which is similar to a fabric. She's making sure all of it is strong, with no breakage, and she is so happy. I reminded Carol, that the priest had on a robe of black fabric from which, within the cloth, golden light emanated, and that both are of the fabric of energy and light, as we are all One.

We spoke for a while longer and at the end of our session, Carol left feeling like a new person, an empowered person, and more certain of her purpose. She now knows, no matter what her experience and with whom, she can stand up for herself—knowing who she really is.

Food for Thought

Do you know if you are an EB, IP, an

hybrid, or an abductee?

    Do you know why you are here?

    Have you ever had the feeling that you might be an abductee?

Chapter Eleven

It's not easy being green

In my life, I've lived, I've loved, I've lost,
I've missed, I've hurt, I've trusted,
I've made mistakes, but most of all,
I've learned

A wise frog once said, *"It's not easy being green"* ...

What must it be like to inhabit a body that is different and unfamiliar? We've all put on a pair of shoes that are either too tight, too large, or sometimes give us sores on our feet. If you will, imagine being in the jungle, nearly naked but for a loin cloth, surrounded by people that speak a language you don't understand, living in a place completely unfamiliar to you. Most times within some level of a person, conscious or unconscious, this is how it feels to be an InterPlanetary soul.

Becoming enlightened as an IP soul offers explanation for why behaviors and customs can feel so foreign and can be quite challenging. Before knowing I was an IP soul, I struggled, often yearning to feel connected to those who would understand me, searching for the familiar and yet somehow never quite experiencing it. When I finally discovered and experienced my soul's home, accessing this through a deep hypnotic state, I was then able to let go of these longings and put reason to my emotions. Knowing myself as an IP soul has been both a blessing and difficult at the same time. It depends on what perspective I choose to see myself through my emotion or my purpose.

When I was young, I didn't understand about myself or my cosmic lineage. I now know why I have always wondered, *where do I come from and why do I connect with certain entities or species?* As an IP, I now know it's because they're a part of my lineage, my ancestry. Now I can answer the questions of how I got here, what I'm doing here and how I can continue to fulfill and be a part of the Grand Divine Plan to expand consciousness.

One thing was for sure when I was younger—I felt I was different, I felt I didn't belong here, and I yearned to go "home." I wish someone could have explained to me what this was all about as I was growing up, although some of the plan was for me to uncover and discover.

As a young person, it can be helpful to understand if you are an IP and uncover why you are personally here. As a parent or a part of an IP soul's life, we all can be instrumental in helping a young one feel supported and uncover their personal information.

Children, when they are young, see or hear their guides more easily than adults. After all, they have active imaginations or imagery without barriers. Many times, to adults, it seems they are pretending; I know my parents thought so, but my guides were all real. I actually remember, at age five, how my guides would come with me wherever I went. I would carry on conversations with them in public and was told to be quiet. In fact, most times when it was quiet, you could hear me talking with them.

As the butterfly unfolds and spreads its wings, how does it know where to go and what to do?

On Earth, we mostly communicate through speaking. I've come to understand that my soul's home does not communicate in this manner. We use telepathy, communication through thoughts without speaking out loud. As I understand more about myself, this assists me in understanding my Dharma, the capabilities and gifts I have, and why I'm able to read energy the way I do... it is innate.

It's like being in another country, you are different from the implanting of that culture into you and you implanting into it. This is how we pour into the greater consciousness to expand. All souls are reawakening, becoming a part of the entire circuitry to expand consciousness.

So, as we're all a part of a massive grid system of energy and each a hologram of light, some entities' consciousness who exist outside the Earth grid are so massive that they cannot fit into our smaller consciousness here on Earth. Some of these entities present as orbs, a light shape with no form, which is only a very miniscule part of their energy. They are of a high vibration, having evolved into this aspect.

As I was channeling one day, I heard from one of the entities that is a guide for me. Its name, Megalythicon, is from another world in which it is twelve entities combined, each having their separate character but acting as one. I believe this happens more as we elevate to a higher consciousness. It is of the *Emissary of Light,* a counsel and guardians of the galaxy – it is everywhere. It tells me it is just light; it offers guidance and information for me to share with others.

When I asked it, *"why am I here, what is my purpose?"* It responded, *"You are a scout, one who brings information and will return to us with information. You were chosen as you are well suited for this task. We have given you a gift to do your work. You will feel the energy in your hands, they will radiate. You cannot see it but feel it. It's connected to your mind through your third eye. This energy is a direct connection to you. This is not to be misused and not given to everyone, it is to be used in the proper way. It is to be used for others to understand, to learn, to guide, and share information. This is about perceiving, hearing and knowing the truth. It is like a radio wave, you will see the signals come into your hands, then to the brain. You will know how to use this as it expands like energy frequencies, for healing. It is your decision what you choose to do with your gift. This gift imbued from the council."*

It further stated, *"This energy can heal, and the energy can change on a dime, in a moment, in a millisecond. It can change frequencies and there is knowledge in it."* Megalythicon further stated, *"On Earth you don't have this type of technology. You must be open to listen to it, as your mind blocks it on Earth. You need to receive it, even if you don't understand. Earth beings filter through their egos and brain, it is important to put this part of the mind aside to receive. The mind wants to put reason to everything. Allow the energy to enter your whole being."*

When I channel this magnificent entity, I feel completely loved. The energy I'm filled with is hard to express in words. It is an experience that I want all to share. All can have this experience of self-love by connecting and merging with your Higher Self. When we feel our magnificence, we realize all else is our own illusions.

As I've pondered this information and much more that I've been given, I begin to understand further why I had the experience of losing some of my left-brain capabilities as I mentioned in Chapter One. There are times when I need to only hear the true information and not the stored illusions, beliefs, and memories which aren't always needed, enabling me to be a clear channel. This knowing becomes clearer and more understood as I grow. I feel more connected to my life's purpose and the service I'm to share with others.

Every single thing we experience comes from our thoughts. We combine our thoughts with our emotions, or prayers, or mantras whether positive or negative. Every thought we have is creative and has an impact on the consciousness of the world and universes. Therefore, when we focus our thoughts for positive, we create the world that we truly want. That is how creation occurs. It then can simultaneously multiply when we share in a group.

Our world is now shifting into a more feminine energy of compassion, a part of the Grand Divine Plan. In order to do so, we all must be accountable for every thought and emotion if we want to create positively, realizing how powerful we and our thoughts are. When a negative thought comes to view, realize it and move on – don't waste the energy and give it power.

As I share this next experience, again it is important to realize how powerful **we all are –** both positively and negatively.

Years ago, my friend Pat, who is a nurse and is also friends with another nurse, Karen. Karen is a physically fit woman, about fifty-five years old. She hadn't ridden her bicycle in quite a while and decided to do it on this particular summer day. As she rode along, Karen hit some gravel alongside of the road. She then toppled over her bike, headfirst, landing on the ground. Her husband, Tom, dropped his bike and ran over to her not realizing the severity of the fall. This wasn't good— Karen had been knocked unconscious and, upon waking, she realized she was paralyzed from her neck down. She was transported by air to the hospital where she was a nurse. Upon arriving at the hospital and undergoing further testing, it didn't look terribly promising for her.

About a week after Karen's fall, Pat called me at home one day and explained the situation. I didn't know Karen, but I could certainly empathize with her pain and fear. As a homeopath, I offered to visit her in the hospital and help if I could.

When I arrived, Karen was in good spirits and her daughter was visiting. I had brought a handful of homeopathic remedies with me but would need to assess the situation further. I asked, "What movement are you capable of?"

She had some foot movement and raised her one elbow just a bit off her abdomen, but this was all the movement she could do. After assessing her condition, I mentioned I could give her a remedy, but asked if I could offer some energy work for her healing. Karen agreed—she was also a Reiki practitioner and understood about energy.

Within a few moments, I was able to access and read the situation energetically. The energy told me about when she fell and went unconscious. This was a crucial time because this is where the brain begins to think, and fears push their way to the forefront. I read in the moment of unconsciousness she became fearful of being paralyzed and even of death.

I asked for healing at this time and helped open the channel for her to receive this vibration. I was not the one who was healing her—it was her co-creating with Source or God. Our guides also facilitate healing by helping to expand the mind and open us to access this energy.

Karen then expressed a feeling of floating in water. She shared that she actually was always fearful of drowning and didn't like the water, so this didn't make sense to her. But this was what was coming in her vision. As a few minutes went by, she began to see herself swimming and we all could see her legs and arms begin to move.

Karen said, "This is so relaxing and feels so good, I feel at peace and I'm not at all afraid. I love how I feel, I can move more, and I feel hopeful that I will be able to continue to move freely. This is what freedom feels like."

I admit that I felt this was one of those miracles we sometimes hear about, yet don't completely know how it all works, except that it was the energy transmuting. Karen had a miraculous recovery, and with a lot of her hard work she was able to walk out of that hospital within six weeks and eventually fully recovered.

I share this story, in this particular chapter for a reason. If I didn't experience and understand energy as I am able to, I might not have believed what I saw that day. We are amazingly powerful beings and don't always use our energy for our best interests. I often learn to get out of my head and allow the energy to flow.

Quantum Understanding

Quantum physics relates that energy is a product of consciousness and reality is what you choose it to be. It is said that quantum particles have the ability to appear in two places at the same time, or instantaneously influence each other even when they are half a universe apart. It is possible that a photon or a particle of light, being part of the electromagnetic field, can exist in two possible states simultaneously. An item truly only exists as it is observed; otherwise, it is not only meaningless but simply nonexistent. The observer and the observed are one in this case. These statements put a spin on what we understand and take it to another level, as in Karen's healing.

This can be quite a lot to wrap our brain around. In essence, science says that we as souls being of light particles, these particles are energy and can affect energy from anywhere, from just observing—and can have numerous existence at once.

I'll share a past life I recall, in which this concept is denoted through the regression. Remember, in chapter five I spoke about how a soul can splinter into several aspects in the same time frame, splitting the soul's consciousness on Earth or other realms, in order to gain wisdom to evolve. The above concept is how I interpret this regression.

I began my regression walking down a set of stairs and into the Hall of Wisdom, where I found a door. It was a wooden door with an iron handle. I opened the door and found myself in a cenote. A cenote is a natural pit or sinkhole, resulting from the collapse of bedrock that exposes groundwater underneath. Many are associated with the Yucatan Peninsula of Mexico and sometimes were used by the ancient Maya for sacrificial offerings.

I find myself observing and yet a part of the scene at the same time. I am in the cenote within the Earth and see a young boy of about ten years old. The boy is thin and wearing a loin cloth. He has black hair, a blunt haircut and is dark-skinned. He is speaking a foreign language, but somehow, I am able to feel and understand this. He is speaking to a large giant to the right of him, who takes up most of the entry of this cave. This giant, who feels like a spirit guide, is visible yet not, sort of transparent. The giant is there to help this boy and encourage him to enter the darkness. The boy is fearful to move forward and enter the deep darkness. I can feel his fear as he trembles. This feels to be a ceremony of initiation into adulthood that the boy must enter.

The giant encourages the boy to enter the water, but he does this hesitantly. He begins swimming; but it is a long, dark and treacherous tunnel, splitting into many directions each leading to a different place. Only one tunnel leads outside. He was told from the other boys that the tunnel was filled with demons. After a long time of swimming, exhausted and filled with fear, he determines which way will lead him out of this tunnel. He sees the light at the end where his mother has been waiting anxiously. She is amongst his friends and others waiting to greet him.

He steps out of the water, exhausted, but he made it safely! All are celebrating his victory. They have gathered around him to congratulate him and support him. The chief enters the scene. He has a tall staff; he's wearing an animal skin on his back and sandals that lace up his legs. He also

wears a headdress made from the head of a lion.
I can feel his strong presence.

He speaks to the boy, "You are back, this is
good."

He turns to leave and walks away.

I sense this is a man of few words. The
mother continues to shower the boy with
affection as they leave the platform of the tunnel.
She is so happy he returned and is safe.

I then find myself in the next scene. It is of
the boy, some years later, and he is sick. I can see
he is frail, lying on a bed of straw, in a hut. It
seems he has ingested some poison which is
leading to this illness. Now enters a medicine
man. He too is dark-skinned, tall, lanky and also
has a headdress of feathers and shells. He is
hunched over the boy. The medicine man is
chanting while placing herbs on the boy. The
mother is weeping in the corner. There is smoke

Laurie D. Wheeler

coming from a pot. The medicine man begins
blowing the smoke all around the boy. Within a
while, there is no change in the boy's health, and
he dies.

I'm now in the death scene, in which the
spirit leaves the body of the boy and returns to
an alternate reality. As I am observing the spirit
of the soul of the boy, it is leaving and begins to
float above the body. The mother is sobbing, she
has just lost her only son. I can feel the
attachment of the mother to the boy and her
heartache. She doesn't want to let go. There is so
much sadness and pain. The mother is not
wanting to separate and let go of her son. Yet the
boy's spirit doesn't feel the pain of the illness any
longer and wants to leave and return to its pure
soul, the Higher Self.

At this point, I have come to realize I am
experiencing all of these characters. I am the boy,

the mother, the medicine man and the giant. The only person I'm not experiencing is the chief. As the boy had just come from a most difficult experience both physically and emotionally, all the chief could say was *you're back?* Not only was he an authority figure but the chief of his community. His lack of a heartfelt acknowledgement left me feeling as if this was a menial task and feeling uncared for.

I acknowledge I have split myself into several expressions of my soul in order to experience life from multiple perspectives. As I am challenged through these aspects, I am aware of each one separately and yet as a whole. Whew! Challenging, to say the least, as that's a lot of emotion to process all together.

Seeing life from multiple vantage points helped me to understand each one's feelings, and experience deep compassion realizing how hard that life was. I also felt a sense of accomplishment, which provided me with a greater sense of self, as we must learn this on our own, no one can give it to us. I understand more of why I feel in this life the way I do, revealed through each person's perspective and emotions. We expand our consciousness and vibration when we experience who we are without our illusions, through our Higher Self.

I've shared this regression with you for several reasons. First, as an IP, I've searched to put reason to my burning questions, "Who am I and what is my purpose?" More and more, I have a greater realization of how important it is to be able to answer these questions.

The second reason I share this particular learning experience, is that, as I've mentioned before, some of us are more than one person at a time. For me this was confirmed in a most personal way. The boy's fearful experience of venturing into the unknown, with its challenges, is one I certainly can understand. Many times, I've been fearful to step into the unknown, knowing I have guidance but realizing that I'm the one who must take the step. I could understand the giant, who was my Higher Self, acting as a spirit guide to help me along the path. IPs often are both their own guide and Higher Self, offering yet another perspective for evolved souls. I felt the spirit cared and guided the boy for what he was about to undertake, yet the giant was unattached emotionally. I know that guides truly care for each of us, as they have experienced embodied lives also and now help from a celestial reality.

The medicine man's perspective was to help this boy heal. When he couldn't, it felt as if he was a disappointment.

One day many years ago, I was in the nurse's office waiting for my son who had fallen and injured his knee. As I sat and stared at the medicine cabinet filled with asthmatic nebulizers, I thought to myself, *"If I ever find a way to help people heal, I will share this information with as many as I can."*

I could feel the medicine man's heart, as I have been a homeopath with a strong desire to help people heal, more times succeeding and yet sometimes not, and left feeling disappointed.

The mother and the loss of her child—the pain of losing a child, they say, is the worst pain anyone can experience. I have never actually lost one of my children, but I've come close several times. The anguish one feels never quite leaves you, which can be held throughout life. All of this experience in the regression has served me well, as I've gained greater insight from many aspects.

This has also taught me that we must see the Divine in everyone, and learn from them, even the chief. He may have had too much pride to reveal a softer side of himself, at that pivotal moment, or possibly I was to learn to be mindful of what I don't want to become...a true learning of the heart.

Food for Thought

Have you ever felt different from others?
Have you ever felt you might be from somewhere else?
Have you ever felt a deep longing for someone or a home you have never known?
What glasses do you wear?

We delight in the beauty of the butterfly, but rarely admit the changes it has gone through to achieve that beauty ~ Maya Angelou

Final Thoughts

So, what's it all about?

More than ever, I'm often asked either in conversation or as a practitioner, the questions, "What is life all about? How can I tell if it's my mind or my intuition? Where can I go to find my answers? How do I know and hear my guides? These and others, are common questions that aren't always easy to answer. Many people, although curious to know more, are fearful to expand their reality and would rather remain in their comfort zone, neglecting their authentic self and their helping guides.

I'm reminded quite often as I look around each day that some of the technology we are creating is our future. I do have concerns about the AI (artificial intelligence) movement and how it can deaden our senses. When we look to something of non-soulful origins, I wonder, "*What must it be like to ask questions of a robot and rely on its answers instead of going within myself and seeking the guidance within me?*"

My experience says we are at risk of losing touch with what has always been available to us and how we access it. We are in a time now of no more waiting—we must act because we are all in a changing pattern— *we are the change!*

As we co-create with all that is, what do you wish to create for yourself and for the world you live in?

For over twenty-five years I have been reading energy, and each person I work with, each animal I encounter, each plant or rock I hold, or each sound I hear, continues to teach through the vibration it carries. We must be open to receive these lessons every day. Being aware of subtle truths and taking action can be the hardest part of all. From what I've come to understand, this awareness and subsequent action are the keys to transforming life. All of which often require a change in perspective, intention and patience for serendipitous timing in life's happenings.

Focus – Trust – Courage – Honor – Choice – Action = Empowerment!

I remember when I stood at the magical Inca doorway of Aramu Muru in Peru, some years ago, and I was graced with the presence of three light beings one afternoon. They gifted me the experience and magnificence of knowing my soul. I could feel this in every cell of my body. I radiated a glow in and all around me. As I was experiencing this, they telepathically asked me if I wanted to stay or if I wanted to go with them. I was faced with a most important question. I took a moment and then realized that I wasn't finished with what I had come here to be and do.

So, I'll ask you the questions, as they have been posed throughout the book...***Who are you? Do you know your purpose?***

We were born not to be ideal, but to be real, not to become someone else, but to become ourselves-
Dan Millman

I have included this prayer as these words constantly inspire and remind me of how I am interrelated with all that is, not only of this Earth, but everywhere. This prayer, from the Lakota people of North America, reflects the world view of interconnectedness and Oneness that deserves all of our attention during these difficult times. It teaches us to honor one another and to be in harmony with all forms of life, other people, animals, birds, insects, plants, rocks, rivers, oceans, mountains and valleys, and all that is.

Aho Mitakuye Oyasin... *(pronounced mi-TAHK-wee-a-say)*

I honor you in this circle of life with me today. I am grateful for this opportunity to acknowledge you in this prayer...

To the Creator, for the ultimate gift of life, I thank you.

To the mineral nation that has built and maintained my bones and all foundations of life experience, I thank you.

To the plant nation that sustains my organs and body and gives me healing herbs for sickness, I thank you.

To the animal nation that feeds me from your own flesh and offers your loyal companionship in this walk of life, I thank you.

To the human nation that shares my path as a soul upon the sacred wheel of Earthly life, I thank you.

To the Spirit nation that guides me invisibly through the ups and downs of life and for carrying the torch of light through the Ages. I thank you.

To the Four Winds of Change and Growth, I thank you.

You are all my relations, my relatives,

Laurie D. Wheeler

*without whom I would not live. We are
in the circle of life together, co-existing,
co-dependent, co-creating our destiny.
One, not more important than the
other. One nation evolving from the
other and yet each dependent upon the
one above and the one below. All of us
a part of the Great Mystery.*

*Thank you for this Life.
And so it is....*

Symbols

I have included these symbols, which were given to me during channeling, for the purpose of healing and further understanding. I am told they are universal with extensive meaning. We may use these in our meditation, under our pillow or above our head as we sleep or in any fashion to expand or heal. All of this information, and more, can be delivered through your intention. The following information is my understanding for the representations of these two symbols.

These symbols are to be experienced as they are of a vibrational frequency and each are a code. They are given to enhance growth, to learn and evolve to be more of who we are. Spending time using them brings us closer to this point. As neural patterns in the brain fire, they strengthen our thoughts each time. Nerve cells that fire together, wire together. These symbols allow for us to introduce new concepts and new processes within ourselves.

These are amongst the oldest geometric symbols. The *pi* symbol is unique. It is a mathematical 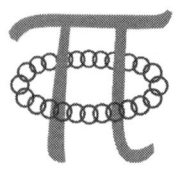 calculation, it is infinite, irrational and can't be described in a fraction. Biblically, it's a symbol for the meaning of life... The numbers of *pi* act as uniting bridges and are foundational. The equation for *pi* is incorporated into many sites. The Giza Pyramid is one of them and was built with the knowledge of this value.

It is a universal language and the platform all is built on, that Source created and deciphers information in the spirit world. Many natural phenomena reoccur with this mathematical consistency. These numbers are encoded into our words and are a way to access messages. *Pi* is found in geometric equations, trigonometry, and the fundamental interactions of nature – it is electromagnetic. All of technological innovations incorporate this sacred number.

The symbol of *pi,* within the linked rotating circle, is an expression of infinity contained within creation itself. Each circle, as is the chain, is connected to each other, there is no separation. The vibration of the chain holds the energy of forever and being united as One. The circle is the most perfect of creative forms, without beginning or end, without sides or corners. It stands for illumination, enlightenment and perfection in unity. As a healing symbol which is used to clear the mind, increase the connection with the Higher Self, and improve learning and communication abilities. ·

The chain encompasses *pi*, which holds a totality, wholeness, original perfection, the Self, the infinite, eternity, timelessness, God, Source or Creator, as the circle whose center is everywhere. Its healing properties extend through the experience of ourselves as One.

Triangles are found in ancient symbolism and ruins dating back to the earliest civilizations.

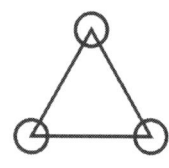 Due to the fact that triangles contain three corners and three sides they are often linked to different trinities. Past present and future, mind, body & spirit, physical, mental and emotional etc... The triangle is inseparable from the number three.

As one represents force, and two

represents an opening, then *three* is the birthing and a doorway of true wisdom. The combination of polarities can provide a new opening, balancing thought and emotion, then providing a doorway to higher wisdom. This is a major teaching tool in symbolic learning. As the circle is a symbol dating back to ancient civilizations, the triangle intersecting the circle and pointing upward, depicts a strong foundation or stability. All lines lead back to the circles. This is like a dance of sound – color – and numbers. It translates into vibration and harmony, the universal communication. When the mind knows and loves itself, there is a trinity, a trinity of knowledge, love and awareness.

I have included larger images of these symbols for you to use as you wish in the following two pages.

Laurie D. Wheeler

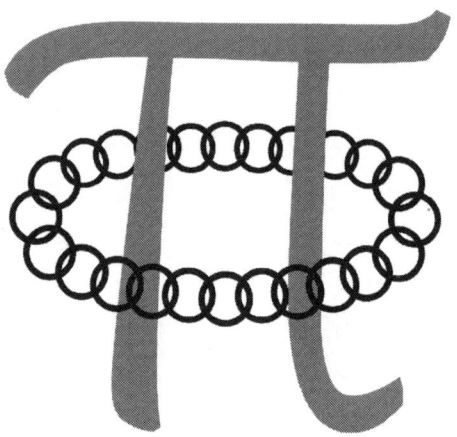

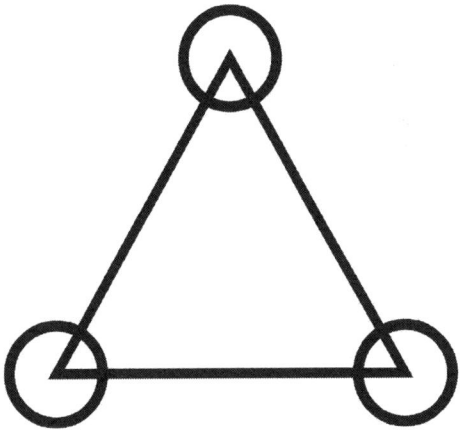

Acknowledgments

I would like to acknowledge three master teachers, each individually who have been an inspiration to me over the years. I feel privileged to have taken classes with each of them, learning the wisdom and knowledge of their craft they share, thereby, influencing my work.

Dr. Linda Backman, a psychologist, brings her amazing knowledge about Past Life and Between Life Soul Regression, sharing compelling glimpses of the soul and its evolution, through the regression sessions she facilitates and passes on to her readers.

Dr. Hank Wesselman, an anthropologist teaches us through the many books he's written, one of which is my favorite, The Bowl of Light. This book shares a rare and intimate glimpse into the teachings of a Hawaiian Kahuna, Hale Makua, as Hank was gifted the sacred knowledge of the ancient Hawaiians. This book holds a special place in my heart, having lived on the Big Island of Hawaii, through these teachings, I feel a deep connection to this Hawaiin Elder and the Hawaiian wisdom.

Sandra Ingerman, MA is the author of twelve books and is truly a master teacher in the study of Shamanism. In her books and classes, Sandra conveys her teachings with an open, kind and compassionate heart, inspiring us through ancient traditions and bridging these healing methods into our contemporary society.

Author Biography

Laurie D. Wheeler's highest mission is to work with the principles of true healing and the energy force it seeks to transcend. In her holistic approach, she uses several therapeutic modalities, such as homeopathy, gemmotherapy, energy work, shamanism and Past Life and Between Lives Soul Regression. These modalities enable her to become in touch with her client's mind, body and soul, thereby, helping to restore a balance of the whole person.

Laurie has extensively worked with and taught people of all ages, presenting information at a level of comprehension with real-life examples, inspiring personal power, passion, truth, strengths and motivation – *the juice for purposeful living.* She is adept as an educator and visionary, facilitating individual sessions, group workshops and major conference seminars.

Her business acumen stems from several entrepreneurial endeavors, one of which was creator and host of a live radio program called *Journey into Wellness,* bringing forward different modalities to broaden the knowledge of mind and body understanding to the community. In 2009, Laurie founded a non-profit holistic health clinic for military service people, aiding those unknown to the world of holistic medicine. She has also been a consultant and teacher of homeopathy for the York Wildlife Center, who now use it as their first form of medicine to aide non-domesticated animals.

Laurie is married to her husband, Bob Wheeler, with four children and has one married daughter with two grandchildren.

For further information, classes or a personal session, please visit www.WellnessWithin.net or contact Laurie at homeopathy2@aol.com.

Suggested Reading

Dr. Linda Backman:
Bringing Your Soul To Light
The Evolving Soul
Souls On Earth: Exploring Interplanetary Past
Lives

Dr. Hank Wesselman:
Bowl of Light
Spirit Medicine
Visionseeker
Medicinemaker
The Spiritwalker Teachings
and more...

Sandra Ingerman:
Awakening to the Spirit World
Soul Retrieval
Shamanic Journeying
Walking in Light
The Book of Ceremony

Speaking with Nature
Medicine for the Earth
and more...

Dan Millman:
Way of the Peaceful Warrior
Sacred Journey of the Peaceful Warrior
The Hidden School
and more...

Gregg Braden:
The God Cocde
Human by Design
and more...
Deepak Chopra
The Seven Spiritual Laws of Success

Michael Newton, Ph.D:
Memories of the Afterlife
Journey of Souls

Neale Donald Walsch:
Conversations With God
The Celestine Prophecy

Don Miguel Ruiz:
The Four Agreements

Pema Chodron:
When Things Fall Apart

Anita Moorjani:
Dying To Be Me

Laurie D. Wheeler

Oh, no! Not Another Learning Experience!

Made in the USA
Columbia, SC
06 December 2020